CONTENTS

INTRODUCTION

No subject is more mysterious than why we dream. Dreams are mysterious because we don't understand them. In view of this, many people have questioned whether God is behind our dreams. Yet few pastors preach sermons about dreams. Still, throughout the Bible, God spoke to people in dreams. Some of these spiritual dreams changed the destinies of nations, whereas other divine dreams foretold the birth of Christ.

No doubt you can recall a dream from your past that was vivid and unforgettable, and you asked the question: Was that dream from God? If so, how would you discern the meaning of that dream? There is a book that has a lot to say about dreams. That book is the Bible. One verse that speaks to our times loud and clear is Acts 2:17: "And it shall come to pass in the last days, says God, that I will pour out my Spirit on all flesh: Your sons and daughters shall prophesy, your young men shall see visions, your old men shall dream dreams." By any interpretation, the Lord is not speaking about normal dreams here.

There are many questions people have about the Bible, but none more puzzling than God using dreams to reveal messages to people. Throughout the Bible, there are stories of how God warned, prepared, and revealed events to individuals through dreams. So why would the creator of the universe use dreams to communicate his will? After all, he is God. And if one acknowledges the awesomeness of God, why would he use dreams to convey his will?

Some Christians will argue if you know your Bible and have the Holy Spirit living inside you, why would God speak to you through dreams? Granted, the Bible does not fully explain why God uses dreams, but nothing written in the New Testament would suggest God no longer uses dreams to reveal messages to us. Thus, perhaps God designed something within our subconscious to recognize his voice through dreams.

The strongest passage in the Bible that supports this contention can be found in Job 33:14–16: "For God may speak in one way, or in another, Yet man does not perceive it. In a dream, in a vision of the night, When deep sleep falls upon men, While slumbering on their beds, Then He opens the ears of men, And seals their instruction."

In many ways, this passage confirms the use of dreams by God to communicate his will to us. If so, by embracing our spiritual dreams, we're submitting our will to that of God's.

Chapter 1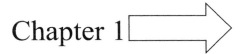

A Dream

Dreams and trying to understand them are two experiences all people share. Yet despite all the research concerning dreams throughout history, one thing remains true: dreams are mysterious. Dreams are mysterious because they cannot be explained. That fact along with the personal nature of our dreams is the reason we ponder the question: Is God behind our dreams?

The dictionary definition of a dream is "a series of images or thoughts in the mind of a person asleep." No doubt you have asked the question that I have asked many times: Why did I have that dream? Often our dreams concern some stress or situation we're going through. Stress at work, concerns for our children or spouse, or unforeseen events are all possible explanations for a dream or series of dreams.

Unusual dreams can also occur after watching something violent or explicit. Still, most people can connect the dots between a bad dream and something they watched or experienced. Despite this, there are times when those dots cannot be connected. When those times occur, they are left wondering about their disturbing dreams.

All people dream, but at different levels and intensity. Like many people, I was always curious about my dreams, but I never gave them much thought. Although I did have a dream in my twenties that was prophetic. I dreamt my wife was pregnant. Despite this, I did not feel compelled to pray about it or ponder its meaning. Instead, I disregarded this dream as an odd coincidence.

On average, most people will experience three to six dreams a night. Yet they won't remember them, and nobody can explain why. Granted, some people take medication, which hinders their sleep levels because these drugs can affect brain activity while sleeping. This is especially true for veterans on medication for anxiety, depression, and PTSD (post-traumatic stress disorder). As a result, they cannot enter the deepest stage of sleep, which is REM (rapid eye movement). Thus, they don't dream consistently.

I heard this often during counseling sessions with soldiers returning from deployments to Iraq and Afghanistan. This had a profound effect on their moods, which affected every aspect of their life. Even those soldiers who could dream often had nightmares regarding their deployments. Thus, they could never experience restful sleep. As a result, they struggled with adjusting to civilian life after leaving the military.

Dream Messages

Most people would agree that dreams are personal. So if you are married or in a close relationship with someone, you may share an unusual dream with that loved one. Conversely, what if that dream was disturbing or unexplainable, would you still be willing to share that dream with a loved one? Further, what if that dream was a warning or revelation concerning someone you loved or trusted? Would you still be willing to expose yourself to possible criticism or rejection over a dream?

To understand a dream and share it with someone, you must remember it. And almost without exception, your nightly dreams fade from your memory once you wake up; although a nightmare may linger longer in your mind, especially if that nightmare woke you up. But most of your nightly dreams simply vanish from your memory.

This is puzzling because we remember things best when there are pictures associated with them. And dreams are a sequence of mentalimages or pictures as you sleep. So based on how we remember things, best dreams should be easy to remember, but they are not.

No doubt sleeping well, and dreaming is important for our physical, mental, and spiritual health. One could go several weeks without eating food, perhaps three days without water; however, just missing one night's sleep will instantly affect every aspect of your health. Many people, however, will sacrifice the number of hours they sleep to get things done. Ultimately though, those lost sleep hours will cause one to break down physically and emotionally. So if one is physically and emotionally tired, this will affect their spiritual health too. As a result, they may not be receptive to the urges of the Holy Spirit.

Given this, no doubt God is revealing things to people through their dreams. Since people today are distracted and overwhelmed by life. As a result, Christians are anxious and not focusing on God for answers. Whereas nonbelievers are focusing on secular solutions to solve spiritual problems. Thus, neither Christians nor nonbelievers are trusting God with their problems.

One could argue if God wanted to tell you something, why not just tell you? Still, like many aspects of God's nature, there is no short answer to explain why. The famous adage "his mysterious ways" is the best answer I can give to explain God's ways. So the fact that God would use dreams to speak to believers is puzzling, but he does so with nonbelievers too. This seems to conflict with the view that some Christians hold that God has nothing to do with nonbelievers. Conversely, nonbelievers throughout the Bible were moved to change course after receiving dreams from God.

If sleeping well and dreaming are necessary for our overall health, God, who created us would have addressed the matter in the Bible. A passage in Job 33:15–16 addresses this issue: In a dream, in a vision of the night, when deep sleep falls upon man, while slumping on their beds, Then He opens the ears of men, and seals their instruction.

God clearly states in this passage the spiritual significance concerning sleeping and dreaming. In addition, throughout the Bible, God used dreams to warn, instruct, prepare, and encourage those of faith.

The Bible is clear about dreams: God will use them to instruct, prepare, warn, and encourage those of faith. Still, one must be of sound mind, body, and spirit to recognize and interpret the dreams of God. Therefore, just like daily Bible reading, prayer, and meditation, we must be receptive to possible messages from God through our dreams. If God never changes, then conveying messages via dreams still applies to us today.

My Dreams

I was not brought up in a Christian home, and I did not come to Christ until I left home and joined the military. The only Christian exposure I had before joining the military was attending a Catholic school for three years. Despite this, I never read the Bible, nor did I understand the Trinity. As a result, once my parents divorced when I was sixteen, I did not attend any more masses or other church services.

After I accepted Christ, I was hungry to know more about the Bible, but I had no spiritual mentors to guide me. Shortly after my conversion, I met and subsequently married my first wife. My wife was Protestant, and she attended church throughout her life. Therefore, we attended Protestant churches for the next twenty-two years. Although we preferred conservative churches, we could not always find one in the places I was stationed. Therefore, we attended the best church available.

Throughout my first twenty-two years as a Christian, I had a traditional view of Scripture. In short, I neither understood nor believed in controversial Christian tenets such as speaking in tongues, laying hands on the sick, casting out demons, or receiving prophetic words of knowledge or wisdom. Furthermore, I would mock those that believed in such things. Yet God gave me hints through the years that my theology would change one day; however, I did not recognize the signs.

When I retired from the US Army, I experienced an identity crisis. Although I had a strong faith in God when I retired, my identity as a senior sergeant was stronger. As a result, I started to experience uncontrolled anger that consumed me. This anger led to marital problems. Consequently, after two separations over two years, my marriage ended in divorce. This devastated me emotionally and changed me spiritually.

Shortly thereafter, I started to experience disturbing dreams. These dreams were dark and frightening, but they conveyed symbolic messages that I did not understand. These dreams were so vivid that I was not afraid to share them with other Christians; however, many doubted my dreams had spiritual significance. Even the pastors I approached about my dreams doubted they meant anything. I even had a pastor tell me that dreams are not in the Bible.

Since I was in my forties at the time, I was not embarrassed or hurt by comments from my pastors. Although I always respected my pastors through the years, I knew they were not receptive to other biblical tenets. I knew this because during my military career, I attended many different churches throughout the country. Thus, I found out Christian denominations differ concerning their interpretation of Scripture. Some of these differences were minor, while other denominations taught doctrines that could not be supported by Scripture.

Despite what others thought, I knew there were spiritual messages in my dreams I did not understand. In short, I did not understand the symbolism within my dreams. My eyes were finally opened about spiritual dreams after I researched what the Bible cited about them. Thereafter, I found a blueprint for understanding biblical symbolism within my dreams. This biblical research took several months to complete.

I discovered dreams of the Bible always had a purpose, and many of them included symbolism. Thus, the people who experienced them could not always interpret them. So God would put his servants into positions that allowed them to interpret these dreams. As a result, God would receive the glory and his people would get awarded for interpreting these dreams. Some of these awards helped the Israelites form a nation.

Biblical Dreams

The Bible is the most powerful book ever written, and the most mysterious book ever written as well. Mysterious in the sense that God does not fully explain why he does what he does. Given this, if God reveals the same message in both the Old and New Testaments, then it applies to us today too.

For example, no one can argue that the acts of stealing, murder, and adultery were cited in both Testaments and are still considered sinful practices today. So, can we use the same rationale for controversial topics such as hearing from God via dreams?

There are many questions one may ask about the Bible, but none more puzzling than God using dreams to reveal messages to people. The Bible has many passages citing how God warned, prepared, and revealed events to individuals through dreams. So why would the creator of the universe use dreams to communicate his will? After all, he is God. And if one acknowledges the awesomeness of God, it doesn't seem logical he would use dreams to speak to us, but he does.

We find in the book of Genesis, God's initial dreams to mankind. In Genesis 20:3 the first account of God using a dream is cited. The dream warns of divine consequences for Abimelech because Sarah, Abraham's wife was in his palace. Then in Genesis 20:6–7, God gives instructions to Abimelech to fix the problem.

The next dream in Genesis 28:12–16 is Jacob's famous ladder dream that is symbolic of the countless descendants of Abraham. Other dreams in Genesis are as follows: in Genesis 31:24, we find God speaking to Laban the Syrian; in Genesis 31:11–13, an angel of God speaks to Jacob; then in Genesis 37:6–7, Joseph has a dream about sheaves; in Genesis 37:9, Joseph has another dream, which is about stars, the moon, and the sun bowing down to him. And in Genesis 41:1–7, Pharaoh has his famous dream about a future famine in Egypt. Thereafter, Joseph is summoned to interpret Pharaoh's dream. He does and is then appointed as the second most powerful man in Egypt, and thus the world.

In the book of Daniel, God's dreams take on a prophetic tone. First, in chapter 2, Nebuchadnezzar, the king of Babylon has a disturbing dream about a statue of gold, silver, brass, and iron. None of the king's wise men could cite the dream nor provide an interpretation. Thus, the king was furious that none of his advisors could tell him anything about his dream. So he decided to kill all his wise men, including Daniel. Once Daniel heard the news about the king's order, he asked Arioch, the captain of the king's guard why the king's degree was so harsh.

Once Daniel was told the reason behind the degree, he consulted with Hananiah, Mishael, and Azariah his companions. They prayed about the matter, and Daniel received a vision from God that explains the dream. Daniel then requested an audience with the king and told him the interpretation. As a result, Daniel was elevated to a position of power in Babylon.

In Daniel chapter 4, Nebuchadnezzar has another prophetic dream from God. In this dream, Nebuchadnezzar sees a great tree that reaches heaven—a symbolic reference to his Babylonian kingdom. As the dream unfolds, the great tree is cut down, and its leader, Nebuchadnezzar, loses his mind and ends up in the wilderness eating grass like an animal. Daniel explains to Nebuchadnezzar this is God's judgment against him because of his arrogance and pride. The king is then told that once he realizes God is in control of everything, he will regain his mind and kingdom.

In Numbers 12:5–6, God tells Aaron and Miriam his way of communicating with true prophets. God tells them that his prophets will see visions and receive instructions through dreams. This was a command from God about how he spoke to his prophets. Furthermore, nothing written after the book of Numbers in the Old or New Testament ever rescinded this command. So even though the Holy Spirit was given to believers after Christ ascended to the Father, God never rescinded dreams as a means of communicating his will.

Although the New Testament's main point is salvation through the blood of Jesus Christ, we find in Matthew several verses to support God's use of dreams. In Matthew 1:20–21, an angel tells Joseph not to be afraid to take Mary as his wife. In Matthew 2:13–

14, Joseph again is told by an angel in a dream to flee to Egypt because Herod wants to kill the young child. Then in Matthew 2:12, the Three Kings, who visited Jesus were warned in a dream not to return to Herod.

Later in Matthew 2:19–22, Joseph was told by an angel in a dream to return to the land of Israel. When Joseph arrived in Israel, he was afraid because Archelaus was reigning over Judea. So God warned him in a dream to go into the region of Galilee. And in Matthew 27:19, Pilate's wife experienced disturbing dreams about Jesus, and warns her husband not to have anything to do with him.

Another significant verse in the New Testament about dreams can be found in Acts 2:17. This is a prophecy verse about how the spirit of God will move in the last days: "And it shall come to pass in the last days, says God, that I will pour out my Spirit on all flesh: Your sons and your daughters shall prophesy, your young men shall see visions, your old men shall dream dreams."

God proclaimed this same prophecy in Joel 2:28 of the Old Testament: "And it shall come to pass afterward that I will pour out my Spirit on all flesh; Your sons and your daughters shall prophesy, Your old men shall dream dreams, Your young men shall see visions." These two verses refer to a time when God's people will experience the supernatural.

The passage in Acts 2:17 cites three manifestations of the Holy Spirit, which are different but connected. For example, a word of prophecy means one receives a message from God for an individual or group-- whereas visions are like dreams, but the person is awake. And dreams are a series of mental images while we sleep. All Christians will experience spiritual dreams in their lifetime, but many won't recognize them as messages from God.

The commonality of all three is that believers will experience messages from God that are personal, powerful, and unexplainable. As a result, when one receives a manifestation from God, it forever changes them. Although the church today has access to Bibles, Jesus, and the indwelling of the Holy Spirit, God still manifests himself in supernatural ways. One of those manifestations is through spiritual dreams.

Recognize God's Dreams

A key characteristic of a dream from God is the imprint it leaves behind. For example, the dream will not be forgotten, and the spiritual message for it will become known in time. In contrast, a normal dream will be forgotten soon after waking up. Granted, a nightmare may linger longer in your memory, but in time it will fade away as well. Some believe if you write down your dreams, you will remember them. That may be true, but you'll only remember the facts about your dreams, but the imprint of those dreams will be forgotten.

Another way to identify a dream from God is the message it conveys and the emotions you feel. In contrast, a typical dream is like watching a home movie-- you're there but the intensity is missing. A true dream from God will invoke strong emotional reactions that don't fade away. In short, you'll remember your feelings of fear, panic, or love experienced during the dream. Furthermore, your dream will convey a spiritual message too.

Some of these spiritual messages are easy to understand. For example, you may be told to pray for someone or get confirmation your pastor's sermon last Sunday was meant for you. In addition, I have found that spiritual dreams are filled with symbolism. Because of this, you must understand spiritual symbolism to interpret these dreams.

The Bible is full of symbolism. A lot of the symbolism in the Bible can be interpreted. For instance, the term *sheep* is often cited in the Bible. Sheep is a symbolic term for Christians. Further, sheep are often mentioned in parables and verses to demonstrate biblical principles of care, vulnerability, and the need for a shepherd. In contrast, biblical passages of snakes or dragons are symbolic terms for demons or Satan. Conversely, some animal symbolism in the Bible can have different meanings, such as a lion.

When the Bible mentions a lion, it can symbolize strength, courage, or fear. The fear reference could be an empire, an individual, or Satan, who is considered a roaring lion seeking whom he might devour. In addition, in the book of Revelation, the first living creature looks like a lion. Since the lion can symbolize many different things in the Bible, you must discern its meaning based on the context of the passage you're reading. Furthermore, any animal depicted in a spiritual dream represents a biblical metaphor for you to discern and act upon.

The Bible also uses metaphors to describe characteristics of God, believers, nonbelievers, and spiritual warfare. In John 15:2, Jesus describes himself as the True Vine: "Every branch in Me that does not bear fruit He takes away; and every branch that bears fruit He prunes, that it may bear more fruit." Then in John 15:5, Jesus explains what the vine and branches represent: "I am the vine, you are the branches. He who abides in Me, and I in him, bears much fruit; for without Me you can do nothing." Jesus also is described as light, bread, temple, Lamb of God, and Good Shepherd.

New Testament Dreams

In the book of Matthew, we know that Joseph, Mary's husband, was Jewish. By all accounts, he was obedient and faithful to the teachings and traditions of first-century Judaism. So when Joseph finds out that Mary is pregnant, a moral dilemma confronts him. Because based on Jewish law, he could have had Mary stoned or publicly disgraced. In Matthew 1:19, Joseph makes a decision: "Then Joseph her husband, being a just man, and not wanting to make her a public example, was minded to put her a way secretly." Before Joseph could act on this decision, God intervenes through a dream to ease his fears about Mary's pregnancy. We are told that the Angel of the Lord spoke to Joseph in the dream: "Joseph, son of David, do not be afraid to take to you Mary your wife, for that which is conceived in her is of the Holy Spirit."

Based on this dream, Joseph changed his mind about putting Mary away. The Bible does not mention whether Joseph struggled with this decision. In any event, it did not matter what Joseph felt about his wife being pregnant because this dream overruled his thinking on the matter.

Christians today give little thought or credit to what Joseph sacrificed by marrying Mary. For one, the child Mary was carrying was not his child. And secondly, a Jewish man who was taught the law no doubt struggled with his decision to marry

Mary. Nevertheless, after Joseph received this revelation dream from God, he changed his mind about Mary. Although this dream was for Joseph, it provides us confirmation that God will communicate his will in unconventional ways—such as through dreams.

Warning Dreams

Another reason God uses dreams is to warn us. Warn us about people, a current situation, or a future event. In Luke chapter 16, we are told about the unjust steward. In Luke 16:8, Jesus warns us about people of the world: "So the master commended the unjust steward because he had dealt shrewdly. For the sons of this world are more shrewd in their generation than the sons of light." Nothing has changed in the last two thousand years. So, as a Christian, you will be manipulated and deceived by people you know and trust. Nevertheless, you must continue to be there for people in need, but always ask God for wisdom before helping someone in need. Still, don't be surprised by their ingratitude.

No doubt you could tell me stories of situations you've experienced with family members, friends, and others. Even though we're Christians, it still hurts when people take advantage of us. We can take comfort though, by the verses in the book of Proverbs, which provide us a spiritual compass for living in a fallen world. In Proverbs 4:7, we are told that wisdom is the secret to living well: "Wisdom is the principal thing; Therefore get wisdom. And in all your getting, get understanding."

Wisdom for the believer does not come overnight. Still, there is a proven biblical process that never fails to produce wisdom. That process starts with a trial, followed by perseverance, which produces patience, and concludes with hope. Nobody likes trials but going through difficult situations can provide perspective. Likewise, if you have walked with the Lord for many years, you can attest to your spiritual growth after a trial. Conversely, if you are a new Christian, you'll experience difficult periods in life, but so do the unsaved. The difference for the believer is that God is with you through your trials.

11

A warning dream can also be prophetic in nature. For example, many dreams of the Old Testament dealt with prophecies about future end-time events. In addition, in the book of Matthew, Joseph was warned when to leave and when to return to Israel. Likewise, the Three Kings were warned not to go back to Herod. We associate these types of prophetic dreams with biblical characters; however, believers today are experiencing these types of dreams as well. These dreams will have a spiritual theme to them, and they are meant to open your eyes to spiritual matters.

Spiritual Warfare

Some Christians will argue if you know your Bible and have the Holy Spirit living inside you, why would God speak to you through dreams? Granted, the Bible does not explain fully why God uses dreams, but nothing written in the New Testament would suggest God no longer uses dreams to convey messages. For me, my spiritual dreams opened my eyes to Biblical principles that I did not understand. These dreams changed my spiritual life because God revealed things to me about spiritual warfare.

In view of my dreams, I learned that spiritual warfare is how Satan attacks you by using your flesh, mind, and world against you. So the warning in John 10:10 should be memorized by every Christian::The thief does not come except to steal, and to kill, and to destroy. I have come that they may have life, and that they may have it more abundantly." One view of daily Internet news stories can confirm the spiritual state of the world today.

In Ephesians 6:11–12, Paul declares who our enemy is and how to defeat him:

> Put on the whole armor of God, that you
> may be able to stand against the wiles of
> the devil. For we do not wrestle against
> flesh and blood, but against principalities,
> against powers, against the rules of the
> darkness of this age, against spiritual hosts
> of wickedness in the heavenly places.

Pastors often cite these two verses, but they fail to explain how

12

these dark forces affect Christians. As a result, most Christians are unaware of the dark forces against them, which are preventing them from maturing spiritually. In addition, these dark forces of Satan know how to attack you based on your past, family history, and current spiritual condition.

In reference to spiritual warfare symbolism, we find the strongest verse on the subject in Ephesians 6:11: "Put on the whole armor of God, that you may be able to stand against the wiles of the devil." This verse is often cited during Sunday sermons, but not fully understood by many believers.

Most Christians think of a Roman soldier equipped for battle when this verse is cited. That is a good interpretation regarding how to put on the whole armor of God. What many Christians don't understand is how to use the whole armor of God. This is crucial because engaging in spiritual warfare is serious business. That is the warning of Ephesians 6:11– 12.

Based on the warnings within the book of Ephesians, how can one stand against rulers of darkness? The answer goes back to our Roman soldier. For instance, the shield of our soldier is symbolic of the protection of God. In short, you cannot fight the enemy with your physical strength, intellect, or human abilities. Instead, you must trust God with all your heart, mind, and soul to defend against the attacks of Satan.

The shield represents your faith in God to protect you from the darts and arrows of the enemy. Further, our soldier's helmet is symbolic for controlling your thoughts. There is a reason the Bible tells us to take every thought captive and test every spirit. Because the enemy loves to plant dark thoughts in your mind. So, you must recognize when dark thoughts come up and immediately reject them. Remember, you have the Holy Spirit within you, and the authority in Jesus's name to remove those thoughts.

The last spiritual weapon is the sword, which is symbolic of the Word of God or Scripture. In short, you must know Biblical verses to cite when spiritual attacks come upon you. In Timothy 1:7, we are told about our authority to overcome any situation in life: "For God has not given us a spirit of fear, but of power and of love and of a sound mind." Hence, you cannot rely solely on others to fight your spiritual attacks from Satan. You must be equipped to fight Satan with the whole armor of God.

Although there are many reasons why God uses dreams to convey messages, I would cite spiritual warfare as the principal reason he does so today. The reason is that Christians today are divided over denominational doctrines. For example, some denominations insist speaking in tongues is required for spiritual maturity, while others insist tongues is not Scriptural. Likewise, some churches teach laying hands on the sick is B iblical, while others insist that that gift of the Holy Spirit ended with the apostles. In addition, many Christian denominations are divided about salvation. For example, some churches teach grace alone, while others insist its works coupled with grace.

These are just a few of the many doctrinal disagreements that divide the church. Furthermore, controversial issues such as homosexuality, gay marriage, and female pastors are splitting up denominations. As a result, Satan uses this discourse among believers to keep us fighting among ourselves instead of against him and his demons.

Because of this divide within the church, God is using spiritual dreams to clarify matters. So, Christians need to realize that fellow believers at different spiritual levels are not the enemy—Satan is the enemy. Also, until Christ comes back and establishes his kingdom, Christians will differ on matters of faith and obedience. Still, on Biblical principles that cannot be compromised, there can be no compromise. So when we disagree with a brother or sister on a core spiritual tenet, we love that person as a brother or sister in Christ, but we cannot ignore their sinful behavior.

CHAPTER 2

Interpreting Your Dreams

A true dream from God will be coded with symbolism. Therefore, to interpret your dreams correctly, you must understand what the symbolism in your dreams mean. A symbol in your dream could be a person, animal, object, or act of nature such as a storm or tornado. The Bible is your main source for understating spiritual symbolism in your dreams.

The Bible is filled with symbolism, and often in Scripture when a symbol is used, its meaning will be revealed in later chapters. Given this, if you're a mature Christian and read your Bible often, you will understand a lot of the spiritual symbolism in your dreams. Conversely, if you're a new Christian, you should seek help from mature believers about their insight concerning spiritual symbols. One key point to remember, though, about your dreams: your dreams are God's messages for you. So do not get discouraged if you cannot interpret your dreams right away, and not all disturbing dreams are from God. Therefore, don't assume all bad or disturbing dreams are from God.

The Bible is your principal tool for understanding spiritual symbolism in your dreams. But sometimes, you will experience spiritual dreams with symbolism that is not Biblical. If so, you determine the secular interpretation of a symbol that reveals a spiritual principle. For example, dreams of falling from the sky with no parachute could mean you have no control of your situation or where you're going in life. The Biblical principle here is that God needs to be in control of that situation and your life too.

A tornado is another common secular symbol in spiritual dreams. The spiritual message here refers to a period of trouble coming your way. This period of trouble is either a self-inflicted wound or some spiritual barrier you must cross. In addition, sometimes the symbolism within your dreams won't become clear until years later. Although this can be frustrating, you must wait on the Lord for the interpretations.

Whenever you experience a dream that is filled with spiritual symbolism, ask yourself this question: was that dream from God? If so, you will be able to identify certain characteristics that are common to all spiritual dreams. The first characteristic will be your emotional response during and after the dream. You will be moved by fear, conviction, or joy. On a personal note, I have woken up many times from a deep sleep after experiencing a spiritual dream and immediately started praying about the situation or person in my dream.

The second feature of a spiritual dream is the impression it leaves in your mind. Because unlike normal dreams that quickly fade from your memory after waking up, spiritual dreams are not forgotten. Instead, they are remembered as events you experienced. In addition, spiritual dreams are like mental imprints that never fade from your memory.

The third feature of a spiritual dream is the symbolism within it. In most cases, the symbolism in your dream will have biblical references. For example, you may have dreams about snakes, chains, dark shadows, lions, swords, shields, or helmets. Although some of this symbolism can be terrifying, God is using it to open your eyes about spiritual matters you must address.

Interpretation

Once you have determined your dream or series of dreams are messages from God, you must find out what your dreams mean. The meaning of your dreams will be coded with symbolism. In short, you must know what the symbolism in your dreams represents to understand the spiritual messages within them.

Your primary source for understanding spiritual symbolism is the Bible; however, interpreting Biblical symbolism requires knowledge of Scripture and how to connect verses in different books. For instance, there are passages in the Bible where symbols are mentioned and then later explained. This is especially true concerning Old Testament prophecies such as those in the book of Daniel. For example, the four beasts cited in the book of Daniel refer to four earthly empires.

We also find in the New Testament that many of Jesus's parables were explained to the apostles in later verses. Yet not all Biblical prophecies are explained, nor are all of Jesus's parables clarified. In addition, you will find that some of the symbolism in your spiritual dreams won't have Biblical references. Given this, you will need to research other sources besides the Bible to interpret the symbolism in your dreams.

One excellent source for spiritual knowledge is your church. Your pastor should be the first person you contact concerning spiritual matters. Yet your pastor may not feel comfortable talking about personal dreams, or believe they are messages from God. Granted, there are always exceptions to the rule, but in my forty years as a Christian, I cannot recall a single pastor who spoke about dreams. In addition, most pastors preach on subjects they know and Bblical principles they believe in. Therefore, besides your pastor, you should seek out opinions and insights from church members you trust. You may be surprised to learn that some members of your church have experienced spiritual dreams too.

For many reasons, the Internet has become our research tool of choice. This is true concerning issues of faith too. There are Christian and secular Internet sites that address the subject of dream interpretation. A lot of this information though is conflicting and misleading. As always though, use good judgment whenever you read material on the Internet about dream symbols and possible meanings.

Furthermore, do not get discouraged if your Internet research does not reveal the answers you are seeking. Always remember, if God spoke to you through a dream, he will in time reveal its meaning to you. Although non-Christian Internet sites based on psychology or Eastern religions can be misleading, they do provide universal meanings to many common symbols. For example, if you have a dream about being trapped or controlled by a giant spider, you will find that one universal symbol for a spider is a woman. I interpreted a dream that puzzled me for weeks after reading this interpretation. Therefore, if you know the universal meanings for many common objects, this can greatly enhance your ability to interpret nonspiritual symbols in your spiritual dreams.

The final point to remember about spiritual dreams: use the experience of older Christians in your church for their opinions and experience concerning spiritual symbols in your dreams. Although it's not a common topic of conversation in many churches, you will be surprised by the number of Christians who have experienced spiritual dreams. So do not be afraid to approach people about your dreams.

Although dreams from God are personal, there are some common spiritual symbols that many Christians and nonbelievers remember from their dreams. Some dream symbolism like snakes, lions, and wolves is terrifying. Whereas symbols such as swords, shields, and helmets are puzzling. The good news is that many of these spiritual symbols can be interpreted by studying verses in the Bible. Although dreams are personal, some common spiritual symbols people recall from their dreams are as follows:

Snakes

There is nothing good spiritually associated with snakes. A snake is always symbolic of Satan and his demons. Many people have dreams of being suffocated by a giant snake, while others have dreams of being bitten, chased, trapped, or prevented from moving forward because of snakes. The message of any dream involving snakes is clear: Satan has a spiritual hold in your life. That hold could be an unconfessed sin, a person, or a situation in your life that is preventing you from growing spiritually.

Let me clarify what I mean by sin: acts of disobedience toward God in action, words, or deeds. In addition, if you're controlled by thoughts of anger, bitterness, revenge, lust, or obsessed with anything other than God, you invite Satan and his demons into your life. Granted, if you're saved, Satan must get permission from God to torment you. Yet if you live outside of God's will by rejecting a godly lifestyle, Satan needs no permission to torment you!

Mature Christians know if they have dreams with snakes in them, this is symbolic for Satan or his demons. So a mature believer by praying, fasting, or both can determine why they are experiencing demonic attacks. The key though is realizing that spiritual dreams about snakes are warnings from God about demonic attacks. Furthermore, like many Christian principles and tenets that are not popular today, pastors won't preach on spiritual warfare because it's not uplifting and disconcerting. In view of this position that many pastors have today, you may need help from other Christians who understand spiritual warfare.

Biblical Verses of Note

In Genesis 3:13, we get the first verse that mentions Satan as a snake:

> And the Lord God said to the woman,
> "What is this you have done?" The woman
> said "The serpent deceived me, and I ate."

Based on Eve's statement, she does not know the serpent is Satan. Yet she knows the serpent tricked her into eating the forbidden fruit. Thus, this is a prelude to how Satan will deceive mankind until the end of the age. Likewise, this verse provides us a clue about Satan's nature and his tactics. Sadly, his tactics are still effective today.

In Revelation 12:9, we get an insight about Satan as a deceiver of mankind:

> So the great dragon was cast out, that serpent
> of old, called the Devil and Satan, who
> deceives the whole world; he was cast to the
> earth, and his angels were cast out with him.

Again, Satan is referred to as a serpent and dragon in this verse. The serpent represents the deceptive nature of Satan, whereas in the End Times, Satan will rule the nations with an iron fist.

In Luke 10:19, we are told about the authority we have in Jesus's name over the dark things in the world: "Behold, I give you the authority to trample on serpents and scorpions and over all the power of the enemy, and nothing shall by any means hurt you." The Lord mentions snakes, scorpions, and Satan in the same breath.

This association is not by accident since snakes, scorpions, and Satan are deceptive in nature and strike without warning. As Christians, we need to take this warning seriously.

Wolf

Many people today have favorable opinions of wolves. A lot of this fascination with wolves is due to our love affair with dogs. Also, people have the impression that wolves are simply big wild dogs. Wolves are feared predators that hunt anything they can kill, which include large animals such as buffalo, elk, and moose. When wolves hunt, they do so as a pack. A pack works as a team when selecting an animal to hunt. They attack as a team with a series of bites until the animal goes into shock and then dies. If the prey animal as large as a buffalo, the wolves will start eating it before it dies. In short, the wild wolf is an animal that has earned its vicious reputation.

In the nineteenth century, wolves were hated and feared by everyone in the United States. As a result, they were hunted to near extinction. The main reason people hated wolves during this period was that they attacked domestic livestock. And once a pack of wolves found a herd of cattle or flock of sheep, they would prey upon them continuously even if they had plenty of wild game to hunt. This fact and their lack of fear for man gave the wolf a nasty reputation through the years as a vicious killer of the defenseless-- a reputation the Old World of Europe gave the wolf centuries earlier.

The reputation of the wolf was well established during the days of Jesus as well. Jesus often compared nonbelievers to wolves. Jesus's analogy here is that the ungodly will take advantage of people of faith. They do this through deception, which is meant to cover up their true or evil intentions. The message is clear: keep your guard up when associating with ungodly people because their actions are never what they seem. Even when you have a friendship with a nonbeliever, you must remember their true nature is controlled by the flesh not the Holy Spirit.

Whenever you dream of a vicious wolf pursuing you, this is a person used by Satan to pin you down spiritually. This person could be a Christian too. Likewise, Satan is using this person because you don't know the enemy is using this individual for his purposes. Also, the individual involved has no idea their disagreement with you is inspired by Satan. Thus, if you have a spiritual dream with a wolf in it, you need to determine who the wolf represents. Further, you need to discern what this individual is doing that is hindering your spiritual growth.

Biblical Verses of Note

In Matthew 7:15, Jesus compares false teachers to wolves: "Beware of false prophets, who come to you in sheep clothing, but inwardly they are ravenous wolves." So what is Jesus's point in this verse? Jesus's point in contrasting docile sheep to a ravenous wolf concerns our two natures: the natural man (our sinful nature) to our spiritual man. Thus, unsaved people are controlled by their passions and will pursue them at your expense. This is what false prophets do, and a warning for us to stay away from them.

In Luke 10:3, Jesus cites wolves as animals that will prey on the weak: "Go your way; behold, I send you out as lambs among wolves." Jesus is not implying Christians are helpless lambs that have no defense against Satan. Instead, Jesus is telling believers they need a good shepherd (him) to watch over them. In short, trust God for protection from Satan and nonbelievers, which wish them harm.

In Acts 20:29, Jesus warns his followers of future trials they'll face once he is gone: "For I know this, that after my departure savage wolves will come in among you, not sparing the flock." Again, Jesus compares nonbelievers to wolves; however, this reference concerns false prophets among the faithful. These false prophets will deceive believers and cause disharmony within the church. Sadly, the Church today has many false prophets who are leading people astray.

Shield

The shield for thousands of years was used to protect one in battle. A soldier could reflect blows from swords and protect himself from arrows and spears with his shield. The shield was an essential tool to ensure success on the battlefield. In addition, the shield served as a source of identification since every kingdom designed its shields differently. Thus, a soldier could gauge how his army was doing by observing the shields surrounding him during battle.

Men today no longer fight in wars with shields. Nevertheless, we still understand that a shield represents protection. The adage "shield of protection" continues to be used by advertisers to sell their products. It is an effective ad campaign because most of us associate shields and protection with ancient fierce warriors such as Romans or Gladiators. The world still views shields as means of protection literally and metaphorically.

The shield is mentioned throughout the Bible as a means of protection. Although the shield was a literal tool used by soldiers and others during biblical times, it's also cited throughout the Bible metaphorically by Old Testament prophets and the apostles. In short, the shield metaphor means God is your protector. God is your provider-- put on the shield of faith. So when you have a spiritual dream with a shield in it, God is telling you to trust him for your protection, your needs, and strength for whatever you are confronting.

Biblical Verses of Note

In Genesis 15:1, we get the first verse that describes a shield as God's hedge of protection: "After these things the word of the Lord came to Abram in a vision, saying, 'Do not be afraid, Abram, I am your shield, your exceedingly great reward.'" Abram understood symbolically what God meant by "your shield." This also resonates with us today because people still view shields as a means of protection.

In Psalm 18:2, we are provided other attributes associated with God as our shield: "The Lord is my rock and my fortress and my deliverer; My God, my strength, in whom I will trust; My shield and the horn of my salvation, my stronghold." This passage encompasses every aspect of God as our provider, strength, protector, and hope for the future.

In Psalm 91:4, we get a metaphoric passage to describe God's protection over us: "He shall cover you with His feathers, And under His wings you shall take refuge; His truth shall be your shield and buckler." Most of us can identify with a protective hen watching over her little chicks. Also, like little chicks, we are vulnerable to attacks from dark things in this world. Hence, God can cover us from dangers we cannot detect.

In Ephesians 6:16, the shield conveys a means of strength compared to protection: "Above all, taking the shield of faith with which you will be able to quench all the fiery darts of the wicked one." Paul is telling us faith in God is powerful and can repel any attacks from the devil. Although faith is an individual matter, it's still God who gives us strength through faith in him.

Helmet

The helmet throughout history was worn by soldiers for protection in battle. Although helmets were heavy and caused great discomfort for soldiers, they kept them on during battle to fend off blows to the head from swords, arrows, and spears. Soldiers knew any strike to their head without a helmet could be fatal or cause serious injury. Because of this, they did not need to be reminded by their commanders to keep their helmets on during combat.

A helmet is designed to protect the head, the head protects the brain, and the brain is the house of our thoughts. The symbolism of a helmet refers to one's thoughts. We are told in Scripture to put every thought captive. In short, do not allow your thought patterns to block the inner voice of the Holy Spirit. When we give in to thoughts of worry, despair, depression, doubt, fear, or refuse to forgive others we block our access to God. Also, your negative thoughts will hinder your faith. That is why we are told in Philippians 4:8 to meditate on good things like what is noble, just, pure, lovely, and praiseworthy. We are what we think—we think what we are.

When you have a spiritual dream that includes a helmet, God is showing you that your thinking is not in line with his Word. Conversely, the helmet could refer to the way someone else in your family or church is thinking, which is not Biblical. Given this, your job is to meditate on your dream and put all the spiritual pieces together. God either wants you to change the way you're thinking or help someone you love. Once again, if your dream was truly from God, he will reveal its true meaning in time.

Bible Verses of Note

In Isaiah 59:17, a symbolic reference for a helmet is provided: "For He put on righteousness as a breastplate, And a helmet of salvation on His head; He put on the garments of vengeance for clothing, And was clad with zeal as a cloak." Although this passage is filled with symbolism, the helmet is associated with one's salvation and head. The connection between head and salvation concerns one's thoughts and beliefs. Thus, salvation is a mental decision to accept Christ. Likewise, it's a decision to reject ungodly thoughts.

In Ephesians 6:17, the helmet is linked to salvation: "And take the helmet of salvation, and the sword of the Spirit, which is the word of God." Also, this verse mentions the sword of the Spirit, which is the Word of God. So even though we don't get a clear interpretation of the helmet in this verse, we can discern from Paul the helmet of salvation refers to our thinking patterns.

In 1 Thessalonians 5:8, helmet and breastplate are linked symbolically: "But let us who are of the day be sober, putting on the breastplate of faith and love, and as a helmet the hope of salvation." The breastplate here refers to faith in God and love for others. So, the helmet of salvation confirms there is hope in life when we think about God's gift of salvation.

Chain

The purpose of a chain has not changed much throughout history. We use chains for securing, locking in place, or binding something or someone to an object. That object could be a pole, fence, wall, or anything strong enough to keep the chained item or person in place. In addition, chains can vary in size and length.

The most common chain most people recognize is the one we use for our dogs. Yet some chains are so massive they require powerful machines to maneuver them. For example, chains are used to lock navy vessels to docks. Given the many uses for chains, the size of them does not matter. What matters is how the chain is used.

In the Bible, there are many verses about chains. Whenever a chain is mentioned in the Bible, it refers to someone held or oppressed by a power or force. That power could be an empire or demonic oppression. When that force is Satan, he has control of a person because of something physical, emotional, or spiritual from their past. Sadly, the believer has no idea why he is under spiritual bondage. Conversely, the person oppressed by the state knows why he cannot escape his situation. The Bible uses both examples to illustrate its points about chains: one cannot break free from these spiritual chains without the power of God.

Whenever you have a spiritual dream with chains in it, they represent something or someone that is preventing you from growing spiritually. These chains could represent a generational curse or judgment, which has been in your family for generations. Some examples of generational judgments or curses are alcoholism, drug addiction, anger, adultery, or physical abuse. Unfortunately, many Christians are unaware of them and do not understand anything about generational judgments and curses.

Given this, you may be the first one in your family who breaks through against a family curse, which has plagued your family for years. Still, to break a demonic stronghold, the individual breaking it must be saved. So if you're saved, ask God for discernment about your family generational curse, and what needs to be done to break it.

Bible Verses of Note

In Acts 12:7, there's a literal reference about chains: "Now behold, an angel of the Lord stood by him, and a light shone in the prison; and he struck Peter on the side and raised him up, saying, 'Arise quickly!' And his chains fell off his hands." Although this passage refers to physical chains being removed, it also conveys a spiritual tenet. That spiritual tenet is God's power to break any physical or spiritual chains against you. Examples of physical chains could be your health, finances, or lack of necessities. On the other hand, spiritual chains could be generational curses, judgments, or unconfessed sin in your life.

In 2 Timothy 2:9, Paul provides us a spiritual metaphor for chains: "For which I suffer trouble as an evildoer, even to the point of chains; but the word of God is not chained." Paul is telling us that doing God's work may require us to endure hardships. Many times, our intercessory prayers for loved ones can weigh us down emotionally. Yet we must be persistent in our prayers and obedience.

We find in 2 Peter 2:4 a dire warning of the consequences of sin and disobedience toward God: "For if God did not spare the angels who sinned, but cast them down to hell and delivered them into chains of darkness, to be reserved for judgment." Although this passage refers to God's judgment against disobedient angels, Paul's message is clear: there are spiritual consequences for defying God. Even Christians can be guilty of defying God by not repenting of known sin.

Sword

The sword for thousands of years was the main weapon of war. Success or failure on the battlefield depended on how well soldiers could use their swords. The size of the sword did not determine the victor in battle. Instead, it was the skill of the soldiers with their swords that determined who lived to fight another day. Soldiers had to train constantly with their swords until every fighting maneuver became instinctive. Empires were built and maintained because of the fighting reputation of their soldiers. As an example, the Roman Empire lasted seven hundred years because people feared their soldiers.

Ordinary people also used swords during ancient times for protection from bandits and wild animals. So possessing a sword during ancient times provided real and perceived protection for people. Like guns today, swords during ancient times represented different things to different people. As noted, swords in the hands of soldiers represented strength and fear of the state, while swords in the hands of people represented protection and security. Also, symbolically, the sword represented the authority of the king since his words could end your life or start a war.

In the Bible, the sword is mentioned many times. Many verses cite the sword as an instrument of war. The sword is often referred to as the means of war throughout the Bible. It is also portrayed as the means of your protection, defense against the enemy, and your way of life. The sword also refers to the power of God's Word. In short, citing Scripture to a given situation. For example, "In Jesus's name, I pray." Before Jesus ascending to heaven, he told his disciples they could ask the Father for anything in his name. Hence, there is power in using the name of Jesus to get our prayers answered. Likewise, citing Biblical verses in given situations has power too.

If you have a spiritual dream about swords, it does not mean a physical fight with a foe, but a spiritual fight that requires the Word of God. For example, you're using secular means to address a temptation, addiction, or troubled relationship. Instead, God expects you to address the issue through his Word. In short, what does the Bible say about this situation? Furthermore, what are the spiritual steps to follow to resolve the problem?

Biblical Verses of Note

In Genesis 27:40, Esau is told by his father that his life will be one of strife and fighting: "By your sword you shall live, And you shall serve your brother; And it shall come to pass, when you become restless, That you shall break his yoke from your neck." There is nothing symbolic about the sword in this passage. Instead, the sword here is literal. Thus, Esau will have to fight his enemies to live, and he will never enjoy peace. This also applies to nonbelievers who use the methods of the world to get ahead.

We find in Matthew 10:34, Jesus's assertion that following him will cause division and strife for believers: "Do not think that I came to bring peace on earth. I did not come to bring peace but a sword." Although the sword here is symbolic, it still conveys an instrument of war. This war may not be a physical one, but a spiritual conflict. Since Christians are in a state of spiritual warfare against Satan and his demons. Likewise, many unsaved loved ones will cause strife for believers.

Conversely, in Matthew 26:52, Jesus states those who use violence will suffer the same fate. "But Jesus said to him, 'Put your sword in its place, for all who take the sword will perish by the sword.'" The sword in this verse pertains to violence. The message is clear: those who rule over others by fear and intimidation will suffer consequences. And history has shown those states and leaders that ruled by the sword will meet a similar end. This can also apply to individuals who use their positions of power to suppress and intimidate innocent people.

In Ephesians 6:17, the sword refers to the power of God's Word: "And take the helmet of salvation, and the sword of the Spirit, which is the word of God." This verse tells us there is power in citing Scripture. For example, many Christians have been taught to request things from God in Jesus's name. We do this because Jesus told us if we ask the Father anything in his name, he will give it to us— assuming it's in his will. Also, we cite Scripture verbatim when confronting spiritual attacks and difficult situations. For instance, when one feels a dark presence attacking them mentally, they would cite, "I have a spirit of power, of sound mind, and love." Also, they could cite, "Greater is he who is in me than he whois in the world." Point: if Scripture is embedded in your mind, you will use it when difficult situations arise.

Children

The world views children as a form of prosperity or blessing for their family. Furthermore, we see children as being innocent, vulnerable, and in need of our protection. A child's faith is often cited by adults as something they have lost through the years and wish they could regain. So it's not just a child's faith in God, but their faith in people, the future, and their belief that anything is possible. In short, children are fun to be around because they see things in a different light than adults do.

Children have a simplistic way of viewing difficult issues and situations. As parents, we try to answer complicated questions in ways our children can understand-- even though we know our children cannot comprehend the facts about a matter. Many times, children will suggest solutions for tough problems, which appear naïve to us, but there is wisdom behind their answers. As an example, when children are told that Mommy and Daddy are getting a divorce because they fight a lot, they will respond by saying stop fighting, kiss, and makeup. As Christians, we know this answer is Biblical, but we reject it.

When children are mentioned in the Bible, they are considered blessings from God. Children are innocent, pure in heart, and malleable for their parents to train. God is especially concerned with children being taught about him. Conversely, there are dire warnings about the consequences for children if they don't love and fear him. Jesus makes it clear children have a great desire to know the truth. In Matthew 18:14, this point is emphasized: "But Jesus said, 'Let the little children come to Me, and do not forbid them; for of such is the kingdom of heaven.'"

A spiritual dream about a child could have two meanings: the first is an actual birth or adoption of a child, which will be coming into your life. If so, God is telling you to accept this child into your home. Conversely, the child could also symbolize Biblical principles of trust, childlike faith, or innocence because children are persistent when they want something from their parents. So God may want you to be persistent in prayer too and keep asking.

Biblical Verses of Note

Proverbs 20:11 is a verse that describes spiritual conviction to do good: "Even a child is known by his deeds, Whether what he does is pure and right." This verse rejects the messages conveyed by our culture. In short, there are not fifty shades of gray for doing right.

Instead, God expects us to be obedient to his Word when we know something is wrong.

We find in Mark 10:15, Jesus's statement about saving faith versus religion that does not save one: "Assuredly, I say to you, whoever does not receive the kingdom of God as a little child will by no means enter it." Jesus's point is clear: you must sell out to God in heart, mind, and soul because superficial faith won't save you. The only thing that saves you is fanatical faith in God-- even when the world says you're nuts!

In Proverbs 22:6, we're given instructions about children: "Train up a child in the way he should go, And when he is old he will not depart from it." Children must be taught many things, yet the thing they must be taught early is belief in God because children are like magnets when they are young. Thus, they need to be guided and instructed on what to do. If parents fail to instruct their children, others and the culture will shape them.

Narrow Path

When one thinks of a narrow path, the image of a mountain climber tiptoeing on a rocky edge comes to mind. We understand the climber must navigate up and around the mountain slowly and carefully by clinging to narrow ridges and spikes. Likewise, the climber cannot rely on anyone else to complete his climb. Instead, he must carefully drive his spikes into the mountain and then climb slowly upward. So it's the person's faith in his mountain climbing skills that provide him the confidence to ignore the dangers. This is how God expects his children to act when confronting troubles. Unlike the climber though, our faith is in God's protection and guidance. And like the climber, we don't know what our next step in faith will entail. Despite this, we trust God to get us through it.

We are all creatures of habit, whether we admit it or not. We all follow a daily routine and think nothing of it—although we all wish for that dream job or a big break. There is nothing wrong with having a daily routine. The same can be said for how we view things spiritually. For example, if you attend a Baptist, Catholic, or Pentecostal church you will view things spiritually based on what they teach. There is nothing wrong with having faith in the doctrines taught by your denomination. The Bible is clear there will be disagreements among Christians.

The Bible is also clear not to judge other believers who do not share our convictions. Still, obvious sin in one's life cannot be sugarcoated—it must be addressed. So as you mature spiritually, the Lord may reveal certain Christian tenets to you that have puzzled you for years.

Whenever the Bible refers to a path, it means a direction to follow in your life. That direction is where God wants you to go spiritually. This message is outlined in Matthew 7:13–14: "Enter by the narrow gate; for wide is the gate and broad is the way that leads to destruction, and there are many who go in by it. Because narrow is the gate and difficult is the way which leads to life, and there are few who find it." These two verses are a challenge and warning to follow God regardless of the cost.

A spiritual dream about a narrow path means to stay focused on Christ and his ways. Likewise, God is telling you that you've veered off course, and he wants you back on the path he planned for your life. Many times, Christians want God to answer their prayers immediately. Yet if their prayers are not answered positively within a week, month, or year they start to doubt their faith and resume bad habits. As a result, the Lord cannot answer their prayers because of sin and unbelief. So a narrow-path dream is God's warning for you to get back on track.

Biblical Verses of Note

The clearest verse in the Bible about God's path can be found in Psalm 25:4: "Show me Your ways, O Lord; Teach me Your paths." There is no symbolic language here. Therefore, the literal interpretation applies. Thus, we must ask, knock, and seek God's guidance on all matters.

In contrast, we find the negative effects of those who do not rely on God's guidance for daily living. This can be found in Isaiah 59:8: "The way of peace they have not known, And there is no justice in their ways; They have made themselves crooked paths;

Whoever takes that way shall not know peace." Every day the powerful, famous, and ungodly succumb to this fate. Yet they do not change their ways.

Tree

In North America, we view trees vastly different than those born in the Middle East. In North America, trees are viewed as part of nature, the woods, or something we see at camping sites. And for the most part, we do not consider trees as our food source.

In the Middle East, however, not only are trees different in size and appearance, but they are valued by people as a source of food and blessing to those farmers who grow and harvest them.

In addition, during biblical times, Jesus compared one's godly character based on the type of fruit they produced. People of his day understood he was speaking of good trees, which produced good fruit, and those that do not. As Westerners, we do not grasp the significance of trees that produce good versus bad fruit. But for those who live in the Middle East, Jesus's parable still resonates with them.

In the Bible, trees are also mentioned symbolically. Jesus, for example, refers to himself as the "Tree of Life." We find in the book of Matthew, Jesus used symbolic language about tree fruit to describe his people compared to those of Satan. This is recorded in Matthew 17–20:

> Even so, every good tree bears good fruit,
> but a bad tree bears bad fruit. A good tree
> cannot bear bad fruit, nor can a bad tree bear
> good fruit. Every tree that does not bear good
> fruit is cut down and thrown into the fire.
> Therefore by their fruits you will know them.

Although symbolic language is used here to describe true believers compared to false ones, Jesus's message is clear: true believers will produce works that demonstrate the character of Jesus Christ.

In view of biblical symbolism about trees, what would a spiritual dream about them mean? A spiritual dream involving trees could have three possible meanings: The first tree interpretation may refer to people in your church or life, and the fruit or works they are doing for Christ. The healthy trees are those that produce good fruit as Christians, whereas those trees that appear dead and dark represent unsaved people. The second tree interpretation could represent Jesus Christ (the Tree of Life). If so, God is telling you to focus on Jesus despite the storms in your life. Conversely, the third tree interpretation could represent a period of rest. For instance, you may experience a picturesque dream of nature on a spring day and feel peaceful. This is God's message to you that a period of peace is coming your way.

Biblical Verses of Note

The strongest passage in the Bible that refers to people as trees is recorded in Matthew 7:17: "Even so, every good tree bears good fruit, but a bad tree bears bad fruit." Although this is symbolic language, there is no doubt what Jesus meant here: unsaved people cannot do works that matter to God, whereas those who know God do works that produce results for God.

In contrast, we find in Peter 2:24 a biblical metaphor for Jesus's death on the cross: "Who Himself bore our sins in His own body on the tree, that we, having died to sins, might live for righteousness— by whom stripes you were healed." The tree here represents the sins of mankind and Jesus's willingness to die to save us.

Lion

The lion is perhaps the most feared wild animal known to man. We fear lions because they can kill us instantly and violently, and we have no defense against their attacks. Although there are many dangerous animals in the world that can kill people, the thought of being killed by a lion and then eaten terrifies us.

We also fear lions because they are big, powerful, ferocious, and fear nothing. Conversely, we admire the strength, majesty, and aura male lions show while patrolling their territory. In ancient times, rulers would punish their enemies by throwing them into a den of lions. For example, Rome at its worst used lions to kill Christians. Ancient rulers used lions as a form of execution because they produced extreme fear in the hearts of people. They did this to control people and to intimidate anyone from challenging their authority.

Since lions have always been feared, killing one during ancient times was considered an act of courage. Likewise, for centuries, some African tribes required their young men to kill a lion as proof of their manhood. Later, in the twentieth century, big-game hunters wanted to test their mettle by shooting a lion. Although many beliefs, attitudes, and opinions on issues have changed throughout history, how we feel about lions has not changed.

There are twenty-five verses in the Bible that refer to lions. Although some of these verses refer to actual lions, most of Scripture cites lions metaphorically. For example, in Genesis 49:9, Jacob refers to the tribe of Judah as follows: "Judah is a lion's whelp; From the prey, my son, you have gone up. He bows down, he lies down as a lion; And as a lion, who shall rouse him?"

And throughout the Old Testament, kings and prophets described kingdoms and wars as fierce lions that roar and devour their prey. There are also prophecy verses citing the lion. For example, in Daniel 7:4, we are told that the first beast was like a lion and had eagle's wings. And in the book of Revelation, the first living creature in the "Throne Room of Heaven" looked like a lion. In 1 Peter 5:8–9, Satan is described as a roaring lion: "Be sober, be vigilant; because your adversary the devil walks about like a roaring lion, seeking whom he may devour. Resist him, steadfast in the faith, knowing that the same sufferings are experienced by your brotherhood in the world."

For us today, comparing our enemy as a roaring lion seems farfetched, but in Peter's day, this metaphor was powerful. Unfortunately, most Christians miss the point of 1 Peter 5:8–9. The point is that Satan is vicious, nasty, and wants to destroy you. There is nothing benign concerning his intent toward Christians:

> The thief does not come except to
> steal, and to kill, and to destroy. I have
> come that they may have life, and that
> they may have it more abundantly.
> (John 10:10)

Since there are so many different things that lions could symbolize in your dreams, you may have to wait on God for the interpretation. The interpretation may come while reading Scripture, hearing a sermon, or through a conversation with another Christian.

Although God uses symbolism in our dreams to illustrate points, he also personalizes them for you. Given this, if there is nothing in your past that pertains to a lion, then it could represent Satan or one of his demons that will be attacking you. Remember, if the lion represents Satan, God is allowing this attack to strengthen you for his purposes down the road. If so, do not be afraid because God has given you a spirit of power, of sound mind, and love.

CHAPTER 3

Secular Symbolism

Y ou will experience spiritual dreams that include secular symbolism. Yet this secular symbolism will convey Biblical messages. Often, nonbelievers will experience these types of spiritual dreams because they don't understand Biblical symbolism. Therefore, dreams about snakes, wolves, or swords won't resonate with nonbelievers. Conversely, dreams that show one is falling, lost, or being pursued by dark shadows can resonate with nonbelievers.

Another aspect of secular symbolism is universal meanings for words or objects. For example, terms such as *black widow, cutthroat, Brutus*, or *weasel* have real and fabled meanings. Further, objects like doors, bridges, and tunnels have real and symbolic meanings to people. Many times, nonbelievers will remember these secular symbols from their spiritual dreams. As a result of these dreams, nonbelievers can be motivated to search for answers for them.

Even though many secular symbols are not listed in the Bible, they often convey spiritual truths. In view of this, you need to determine if an object or natural event relates to a Biblical principle. Likewise, sometimes secular symbols have historical or folklore meanings that convey spiritual truths. Even common adages like

"What goes around comes around" relates to the Biblical passage of what you sow, you shall reap. Thus, when you experience a spiritual dream that reveals secular symbolism, determine if there are Biblical principles for these symbols.

Like Biblical symbolism Christians remember from their dreams, nonbelievers will recall certain symbols from their dreams too. Likewise, sometimes God will use objects from one's past to convey messages. Since many people can recall events from their past based on what they have seen or experienced. God's purpose is to get one's attention. Thus, disturbing dreams about storms or dark figures can urge people to search for answers for them. Many times, those answers come from Christian friends or family members.

Biblical symbolism within dreams is limited; however, secular symbolism within dreams is endless. Despite this, there are some common secular symbols nonbelievers and Christians remember from their dreams. The factor that connects some of these secular symbols is the Biblical messages they convey. In short, there are spiritual tenets associated with these symbols. Some common secular symbols within dreams are as follows:

River

Even today with all our technology, we still value rivers as natural resources that benefit us in many ways. Likewise, in many Third World countries, rivers are essential for water, irrigation, and commerce. Because of this, many people in the Third World have attached religious significance to them. The main spiritual tenet of this worship is that rivers are alive, and they provide water and substance to all; therefore, they need to be respected and worshipped. The Bible, in contrast, does not exalt rivers or any other parts of nature above God. In short, we can admire and appreciate God's natural creations, but never worship them in any way.

There are stories in the Bible about people crossing bodies of water. The most famous story is when God parted the Red Sea so the Israelites could cross and escape from the Egyptians. In addition, when Israel was ready to cross over to the Promised Land, God stopped the Jordan River from flowing so the Israelites could cross over. On the surface, these stories of water crossings do not appear to have clear spiritual messages. However, in both stories, the people had to trust and obey God by stepping out and walking on the sea or river floors. No doubt the people were fearful as they walked across these water beds, but their faith in God was stronger than their fear of the situation. Thus, the spiritual lesson of these stories was faith and trust in God despite the obstacles they confronted.

In view of this, dreams about crossing bodies of water refer to spiritual transformations. A spiritual transformation changes one's maturity, but only after they endure a period of testing. In short, after they finish this period of pruning, they'll emerge out of it stronger in faith, and be prepared to do God's work. They should not fear or dread this transformation. Instead, they should be thankful God has decided to use them for his purposes.

Spider

Many people fear spiders. And certain types of spiders like black widows are poisonous. Yet most spiders are not harmful to humans. In view of this, why do we fear spiders? The principal reason is their physical appearance: they have eight legs; they look scary and trap their prey with webs and ambushes. And though their webs are magnificently designed, they are deadly snares to the creatures that get trapped inside them. In many ways, spiderwebs are beautiful to view, but their purpose is deception. Perhaps the notion of being trapped in a web as our killer is closing in scares us. As a result, we associate spiders with darkness and evil intentions.

In literature and legend, the name Black Widow was given to women of deception. Most of these women were physically beautiful, but they intended to deceive, kill, or destroy someone for their gain. Unfortunately, by the time the victim recognized the deception, it was too late. Men were usually the victims of these Black Widow women. And most of these men were deceived, whether they were strong or weak, rich or poor, handsome or ugly.

The only warnings they received were from other women who could sense the deception.

When you experience a spiritual dream about spiders, this could mean someone you know is deceptive and has dark motives toward you. The size of the spider in your dream can provide clues about the culprit. Thus, a large spider could represent a person of power and influence over you. Once again, spiders symbolically refer to women of deception.

Given this, if you're a man and your wife or girlfriend has a dream about you trapped by a spider, this means a woman has dark intentions toward you. Those intentions are not necessarily seductive. Instead, they could be a desire to destroy your career or ministry. Conversely, when a man has a dream about a spider, this too represents a woman of deception; however, it may be a person in your family who is manipulating others to get her way. On a personal note, I had a disturbing dream about a large spider that represented a family member who was controlling and manipulating others. Although I did not understand the dream at first, in time the interpretation was revealed.

There is no clear Biblical tenet associated with spiders; however, there are three passages in the Bible about spiders. All these passages are symbolic. We find in Isaiah 59:5–6 verses that describe spiderwebs as traps of deception by evil men:

> They hatch vipers' eggs and weave the spider's
> web; He who eats of their eggs dies, And
> from that which is crushed a viper breaks
> out. Their webs will not become garments,
> Nor will they cover themselves with their
> works; Their works are works of iniquity,
> And the act of violence is in their hands.
>
> This passage refers to the ungodly and how
> their evil ways are like snakes and spiders.

Storm

People around the world view major events and natural disasters differently. The Western World, for example, view things vastly different from those of the Third World. For instance, the people of India believe cattle are creatures that need to be revered and worshipped not eaten-- even though millions in their country suffer from hunger. Whereas people in the West view cow worship in India as irrational thinking.

Likewise, the Muslim world views Western society with disdain because of its materialistic nature. Thus, it's extremely hard for the whole world to agree on one interpretation for a given event. A storm, however, means the same thing to anyone in the world. An act of nature that is dangerous and something that can cause death and destruction to life and property. Also, one needs to be prepared for and take cover before a storm.

We, therefore, associate the term *storm* with chaos, uncertainty, danger, and potentially fatal to one's life. Metaphorically, the adage "one stormed out" is an image we can identify with and understand. So, neither a natural storm nor an emotional outburst is something we want to experience.

A spiritual dream about a storm or pending one could be God's warning for you to prepare. This storm will be a period or event that will shape your spiritual maturity. Furthermore, God is telling you to prepare for this storm. Unfortunately, there is no easy way out. You must go through this difficult situation. As always though, you are not alone because God is with you. As someone who has been a Christian for over forty years, I can attest that every storm I've endured increased my faith greatly. Conversely, I never understood the purpose of the storm while in it.

Although pastors often talk about the storms of life, they don't cite biblical verses that refer to storms directly. Instead, they cite other verses that address troubles Christians will experience in the world. Yet there is one story in the Bible that associates storms with faith and trust in God. We find this in Mark 4:37–40:

> And a great windstorm arose, and the waves
> beat into the boat, so that it was already

filling. But He was in the stern, asleep on a pillow. And they awoke Him and said to Him, "Teacher, do You not care that we are perishing?" Then He arose and rebuked the wind, and said to the sea, "Peace, be still!" And the wind ceased and there was a great calm. But He said to them, "Why are you so fearful? How is it that you have no faith?"

In many ways, this story illustrates true faith in Christ against all odds. It also shows how a natural event can convey a spiritual tenet.

Dark Figures

Many Christians and nonbelievers often have dreams about dark figures. Furthermore, most Christians believe dark figures in dreams represent Satan and his demons. Despite this, dark figures in dreams can represent different things to believers based on their spiritual maturity. For example, carnal Christians and nonbelievers may conclude dark figures in dreams refer to dishonest people they know. Thus, the thought they refer to spiritual warfare does not enter their mind. As a result, they are not receptive to God's warnings about spiritual warfare.

Granted, not all dreams about dark figures are warnings from God. Therefore, when one has a dream about something common like dark figures or shadows, they must remember the basics about spiritual dreams: the dream is powerful and invokes strong emotions, the dream is filled with symbolism, and they remember the dream as though they experienced it. If all three elements are there, the dream is probably a revelation from God. Thus, they must find out its meaning.

Once they determined their dream was from God, they must research Scripture for an interpretation. The first Biblical principle they must know: The angels of God are never masked in darkness; however, Satan and his demons can mask as "Angels of Light." Therefore, the dark figure in one's dream is symbolic of something evil. The next step entails a spiritual inventory of one's life. In short, are they doing something that dishonors Christ or destroys their testimony? If not, evaluate one's thinking patterns. Are they consumed by sinful thoughts of revenge, anger, or bitterness toward someone who wronged them? Bottom line: there is something dark hovering over them that needs to be addressed.

Another possibility for one's dreams about dark figures concerns generational judgments or curses. Many Christians have never been taught about generational curses and judgments. As a result, many families unwillingly pass down curses and judgments from one generation to the next. Some common generational curses are alcoholism, drug addiction, violent behavior, suicide, and sexual obsession. And frankly, anything that seems to plague a family could be a generational curse or judgment. The core problem is not psychological or one's environment—it's spiritual.

There are dark spirits behind all generational curses and judgments. In Ephesians 6:12, we are told about the forces against us: "For we do not wrestle against flesh and blood, but against principalities, against powers, against the rulers of the darkness of this age, against spiritual hosts of wickedness in the heavenly places." This verse is powerful and not well understood by many Christians. On a personal note, I was a Christian for almost thirty years before I understood anything about generational curses and judgments.

Although dream imagery of dark figures and shadows could be messages from our subconscious, there must be psychological reasons for them. Hence, there are reasons why we experience weird dreams. Granted, dreams are mysterious and unpredictable, but they are based on our subconscious fears, anxieties, or desires. Conversely, spiritual dreams are not based on subconscious reasons. Instead, they are revelations from God. So if one recognizes the characteristics associated with spiritual dreams, they can determine when they experience one, and then try to interpret its meaning.

Afterthought

The Bible does not explain why God uses symbolism in our dreams. Nevertheless, understanding biblical and secular symbolism is essential for interpreting spiritual dreams. Most Christians will experience spiritual dreams in their lifetime; moreover, some of the symbolism in these dreams will be disturbing. Likewise, many will experience dreams where the symbolism is personal-- since people associate experiences in life with things they have seen. So God may use symbolism from your past to convey a message to you. A message that you won't receive by any other means.

Whenever you experience a dream from God, consider it a blessing and opportunity to improve your walk with him. God is holy, and he wants his children to grow in holiness too. There is a reason God is using dreams now to convey messages to you. Do not get discouraged if other believers are indifferent or amused by your dreams.

I have learned to appreciate and be thankful to God for opening my eyes to spiritual matters through dreams. So even if your pastor doubts whether your dreams are messages from God, don't be dissuaded. Remember, God is not a respecter of persons. All believers have equal access to God if they're obedient. Furthermore, God has used dreams throughout recorded history to convey his will to people. And in these last days, God will pour out his spirit in supernatural ways. One of those ways is through dreams.

CHAPTER 4

Dreams of the Bible

In the Bible, there are many passages about dreams. God used dreams throughout the Bible to communicate his will. Some Biblical dreams were warnings, while others were instructions. Also, we find in the books of Genesis and Daniel prophecy dreams to Joseph and the king of Babylon. God spoke to people of faith and the ungodly through dreams. Furthermore, after these individuals experienced these spiritual dreams, they were prompted to change course because of them.

Many of the dreams cited in the Bible are in the Old Testament. Although in the book of Matthew, we find that Joseph, the Three Kings, and Pilate's wife experienced spiritual dreams too. The only other dream of note in the New Testament is listed in Acts 2:17: "And it shall come to pass in the last days, says God, That I will pour out My Spirit on all flesh; Your sons and your daughters shall prophesy, Your young men shall see visions, Your old men shall dream dreams."

The key phrase in this verse is "My Spirit." God's spirit is the Holy Spirit. So receiving messages from God via prophecies, visions, or dreams are the work of the Holy Spirit.

Although the earliest books of the Bible were written thousands of years ago, God's laws, principles, and tenets still apply to us today.

One reason the Bible applies to us today can be found in Hebrews 4:12: "For the word of God is living and powerful, and sharper than any two-edged sword, piercing even to the division of soul and spirit, and of joints and marrow, and is a discerner of the thoughts and intents of the heart." This passage reveals why people are changed once they apply God's Word to their lives.

If Scripture is truly living and powerful, then verses concerning dreams apply to us today. God used dreams throughout the Bible for different purposes, but there was one common reason for these dreams: to change course. This change course message within Biblical dreams covered many different subjects: warnings from God, deception by others, battle plans, and spiritual errors were all reasons God intervened through dreams in the affairs of people. So by studying the dreams of the Bible, we can understand how they apply to us today.

Some Christians will argue if you know your Bible and have the Holy Spirit living inside you, why would God speak to you through dreams? Granted, the Bible does not explain fully why God uses dreams, but nothing written in the New Testament would suggest God no longer uses dreams to convey messages. For me, my spiritual dreams opened my eyes to Biblical principles I did not understand. These dreams changed my spiritual life because God revealed things to me concerning spiritual warfare.

Biblical Dreams

In Genesis 20: 3–7, we find a warning dream with deception:

> But God came to Abimelech in a dream by
> night, and said to him, "Indeed you are a dead
> man because of the woman whom you have
> taken, for she is a man's wife." But Abimelech
> had not come near her; and he said, "Lord,
> will You slay a righteous nation also? Did
> he not say to me, She is my sister? And she,
> even she herself said, He is my brother. In the
> integrity of my heart and innocence of my

hands I have done this." And God said to him in a dream, "Yes, I know that you did this in the integrity of your heart. For I also withheld you from sinning against Me; therefore I did not let you touch her. Now therefore, restore the man's wife; for he is a prophet, and he will pray for you and you shall live. But if you do not restore her, know that you shall surely die, you an all who are yours."

Backdrop

This event occurred after Abraham separated from Lot and settled in a place called Gerar. Before entering Gerar, Abraham decided to tell the people there that Sarah was his sister. Abraham did this because Sarah was beautiful, and he felt if men knew she was his wife, they would kill him. Because of this deception, when King Abimelech saw Sarah, he wanted her. As a result, he took her to his household because he thought Sarah was Abraham's sister. Abimelech assumed that Abraham would agree to give him Sarah for a price.

This dream demonstrated both God's character and holiness. It also confirmed God's purposes will be fulfilled even when his children failed to show faith in him. In this situation, Abraham failed to trust God for his protection in this new land. Despite this failure, Abraham went on to become the Father of Faith. So this story is a spiritual lesson to remember God is merciful and patient with his children. Conversely, this story shows us God will speak to the ungodly when they threaten his children or purposes. Since God is the ultimate judge, he knew Abimelech's actions were done with integrity. God, therefore, spared any consequences against Abimelech once he returned Sarah back to Abraham.

In Genesis 37:5–7, we find a prophecy dream for Joseph:

Now Joseph had a dream, and he told it to his brothers; and they hated him even more. So he said to them, "Please hear this dream which I

have dreamed: There we were, binding sheaves
in the field. Then behold, my sheaf arose and
also stood upright; and indeed your sheaves
stood all around and bowed down to my sheaf."

Then in Genesis 37:9, Joseph gets confirmation that his
previous dream was from God:

Then he dreamed still another dream and told it
to his brothers, and said, "Look, I have dreamed
another dream. And this time, sun, the moon,
and the eleven starts bowed down to me."

Backdrop

Jacob was the patriarch of Israel and the father of twelve
sons. The descendants of these sons became the twelve tribes of
Israel. Before Jacob was married or had any children, he decided to
work for his uncle Laban. He did this so he could marry his
daughter Rachael, whom he loved. Jacob agreed to work for seven
years to marry Rachael. After he worked those seven years for
Rachael, Laban arranged a great marriage feast for Jacob. Laban,
however, decided to trick Jacob on his wedding night by sending
him his eldest daughter Leah instead of Rachael. The next day Jacob
was upset because he had been tricked. Laban, therefore, agreed
that Jacob could have Rachael too for a wife, but first he had to
celebrate for a week with his new wife Leah. Likewise, Jacob had to
work another seven years for Rachael.

Jacob loved Rachael, but he did not have strong feelings for
Leah. God was upset with Jacob because he would not show any
love toward Leah. As a result, God blessed Leah with children, but
Rachael remained barren for years. As Leah bore sons for Jacob,
Rachael became jealous of Leah and angry with Jacob. Finally, after
Leah bore six sons and a daughter, God decided to bless Rachael
with a son too. This son was named Joseph. When Joseph was
born, all his siblings were much older than him. Thus, Jacob
considered Joseph a gift from God because he was the child of his
old age. This

favoritism toward Joseph by Jacob caused resentment and hate within the family, especially among his brothers.

Joseph's Dreams

We find in the book of Genesis that Joseph's dreams had hidden messages coded with symbolism. Joseph had no idea what the symbolism in his dreams meant. And like all spiritual dreams, they were vivid and powerful. As a result, Joseph wanted to talk about them. Since the symbolism in Joseph's dreams was easy to interpret for his brothers and father, he should have used discretion and not told his family members about his dreams. So by revealing these dreams to his family members, Joseph set in motion a sequence of events that would start his climb to power. A climb to power that would give him authority over his brothers.

There are lessons for us today from Joseph's dreams and his life. The first lesson is God speaks to us through spiritual dreams that are coded with symbolism. Granted, not all dreams from God are filled with symbolism, but many of them will include symbols that need to be interpreted. The second point is that spiritual dreams are meant for you, not others. In short, be cautious about discussing your spiritual dreams with others, because they will not understand your dreams nor believe they are from God. On a personal note, I've had pastors and strong believers express doubt my dreams were from God.

Another key point about Joseph's dreams: the meaning of your dream may not be obvious right away. If so, do not get discouraged because God will reveal the meaning of your dream. And like Joseph, you may be too immature spiritually to understand what your dream meant.

So as you grow spiritually, you will understand more about Biblical symbols and what they mean. Unfortunately, there no set template that can accelerate your spiritual growth. A lot will depend on how sincere you are about serving the Lord. There is truth to the adage "adversity shapes character." Biblical adversity means you have experienced trials and tribulations in life but did not lose faith in God.

In Genesis 41:1–8, we find a dream with symbolic language:

> Then it came to pass, at the end of two full
> years, that Pharaoh had a dream; and behold,
> he stood by the river. Suddenly there came
> up out of the river seven cows, fine looking
> and fat; and they fed in the meadow. Then
> behold, seven other cows came up after them
> out of the river, ugly and gaunt, and stood by
> the other cows on the bank of the river. And
> the ugly and gaunt cows ate up the seven fine
> looking and fat cows. So Pharaoh awoke.

Backdrop

Joseph was already in prison for years before Pharaoh's dreams. He was sent to prison because his master's wife falsely accused him of attacking her. The Lord, though, blessed Joseph while he was in prison. As a result, he had favor with the keeper of the prison. Because of this favor, the prison keeper granted him authority to watch over the prisoners. This position eventually allowed Joseph to interact with the man who would get him released from prison.

The event that triggered Joseph's release from prison was when Pharaoh got upset with his butler and baker. Thus, he had them thrown into prison—the same one where Joseph resided. Since Joseph was responsible for the care of all prisoners, Pharaoh's butler and baker were put under his authority. One day both men received prophecy dreams from God. They were disturbed by their dreams, but they did not know how to interpret them.

Once Joseph was told about their dreams, he interpreted them. The butler was subsequently restored to his duties after three days; however, the baker was beheaded. Before the butler was released from prison, Joseph requested he remember him, but the butler failed to do so. Two years later, Pharaoh had his disturbing dreams. When none of Pharaoh's entourage could interpret his dreams, the butler remembered Joseph. Once Joseph met the Pharaoh, he interpreted his dreams. As a result, he became the second most powerful man in Egypt.

Like Joseph, Pharaoh's dreams were filled with symbolism. Most of the spiritual dreams in the Bible are filled with symbolism. God does not tell us in Genesis why he uses symbolism in dreams, but he does so with people of faith and nonbelievers too. Also, some people are given the gift of dream interpretation, such as Joseph.

In Numbers 12:5–6, God reveals how he uses dreams to speak to prophets:

> Then the Lord came down in the pillar of
> cloud and stood in the door of the tabernacle,
> and called Aaron and Miriam. And they
> both went forward. Then he said, "Hear
> now My words: If there is a prophet among
> you, I, the Lord, make Myself known to him
> in a vision; I speak to him in a dream."

The Lord went on to say that Moses is his special servant. So God spoke to him face-to-face rather than through visions or dreams.

The reason the Lord came down to the tabernacle and spoke to Miriam and Aaron was that Moses had married an Ethiopian woman, and they criticized him for doing so. The Bible does not explain why Aaron and Miriam thought this marriage was a bad move. However, in their eyes, they thought they were just as good as Moses because God spoke to them too. The Lord, however, considered Moses the most humble man in the world. Thus, he was quite upset with Aaron and Miriam for belittling his chosen prophet.

Backdrop

Throughout the Old Testament, God spoke mainly through prophets, not individuals. If God wanted to convey a message to someone, he would use a prophet to deliver the message. Moses, however, pleased God greatly. So the Lord spoke to him directly. This was a special relationship that no one else in the world had with God at the time. Although the Lord spoke to Aaron and Miriam too, it was because Moses needed help with the tabernacle and the people. Yet God's relationship with them was not personal. In view of this, when Aaron and Miriam spoke against Moses, they crossed a line with God. And since Miriam was especially critical of Moses, the Lord inflicted her with leprosy. As a result, Moses had to pray for Miriam, and after seven days, the Lord removed her leprosy.

Throughout the Old Testament, most people did not have personal relationships with God-- even though that was God's original intent for Adam and Eve. Consequently, after Adam and Eve died, only prophets and priests had direct access to God, and their job was to intercede for the people's sins and receive instructions from God about repentance and restitution. Sometimes though, the Lord would send angels to speak to individuals, but most people received their spiritual instructions from priests or prophets. If God did not want to use priests or prophets to convey messages, he would often use dreams to deliver that message.

In Joel 2:28–29, we find confirmation that God will use dreams in the last days:

> And it shall come to pass afterward That I
> will pour out My Spirit on all flesh; Your
> sons and your daughters shall prophesy,
> Your old men shall dream dreams, Your
> young men shall see visions. And also on
> My menservants and on My maidservants
> I will pour out My Spirit in those days.

Backdrop

We know these verses are about the end times because in Joel 2:30–32, we are told of the events that will follow the awesome day of the Lord. Given this, what does the reference to "My Spirit" in Joel 2:28–29 represent? The answer is the Holy Spirit. Because in the last days, the Holy Spirit will draw many people to Christ. Likewise, those individuals saved during this time will experience higher gifts of the Holy Spirit. Some of these gifts will be spiritual wisdom and knowledge. Furthermore, these gifts will be revealed through dreams and visions. Joel 2:28–29 is repeated in the book of Acts as confirmation that God will use dreams in the last days to reveal spiritual messages to his people.

The dream message in Joel 2:28–29 is about prophecy. And when the Bible speaks of prophecy, it's a message concerning future events within one's life or others. Although dreams from God can have many purposes besides prophecy, I believe if you're experiencing spiritual dreams regularly, you'll find that many of them will be about prophecy coupled with spiritual warfare.

You should not dread or fear these dreams. Rather, thank God for his revelations about future events or trials. Granted, some of these events may be situations you would like to avoid. Nevertheless, if God is revealing future events or trials, he will prepare you for them.

In 1 Kings 3:5–9, Solomon is presented the gift of wisdom:

> At Gibeon the Lord appeared to Solomon in a dream by night; and God said, "Ask! What shall I give you?" And Solomon said: "You have shown great mercy to Your servant David my father, because he walked before You in truth, in righteousness, and in uprightness of heart with You; You have continued this great kindness for him, and You have given him a son to sit on his throne, as it is this day. Now, O Lord my God, You have made Your servant king instead of my father David, but I am a little child; I do not know how to go out or come in. And Your servant is in the midst of Your people whom You have chosen, a great people, too numerous to be numbered or counted. Therefore give to Your servant an understanding heart to judge Your people, that I may discern between good and evil. For who is able to judge this great people of Yours?"

Backdrop

The Lord was greatly pleased by what Solomon asked for. As a result, he was given the gift of wisdom. This gift of wisdom was supernatural, and no person before or after Solomon ever matched his level of wisdom. Also, God gave Solomon riches and honor among kings because he was well pleased with him. Solomon achieved a lot for God during his forty-year reign. A significant achievement was the building of the Temple, which God did not allow David to build because he was a man of war. Unfortunately, when Solomon was old, he allowed himself to be influenced by his foreign wives, and he started worshipping foreign gods.

The dream message of 1 Kings 3:5–9 is about choosing between serving God or self. The Lord told Solomon that if he obeyed his commandments and statutes, his days would be lengthened. Although Solomon did great things for God during his reign, he faltered in the end. Likewise, many people today will have spiritual dreams concerning God's will for their life. God will reveal to them a path that they must follow, and if they follow that path, they will fulfill God's purpose for their life.

Like Solomon, though, many Christians will serve God enthusiastically for a season, but when pressure comes from the world, flesh, and the enemy they falter. Because of this, if you have spiritual dreams about following a narrow path, God is telling you not to quit serving him despite all the pressure you're feeling. Remember, you can do all things through Christ who strengthens you.

In the book of Daniel, we are told about the dreams of Nebuchadnezzar, the king of Babylon. His dreams were about future empires and his fate due to his arrogance. Nebuchadnezzar was not a man of God. Despite this, he was given a revelation about the future of the world. These dreams disturbed Nebuchadnezzar to such a point he threatened to kill his wise men unless they could interpret them. None of the Babylonian wise men could cite or interpret the king's dreams, but Daniel could.

In Daniel 1:17, we get an explanation for why God used dreams to convey these messages to Nebuchadnezzar now: "As for these four young men, God gave them knowledge and skill in all literature and wisdom; and Daniel had understanding in all visions and dreams." Daniel's gift of understanding in all visions and dreams would be used by God to promote him and his peers to power in the Babylonian Kingdom.

Backdrop

The Babylonians have just conquered Jerusalem. And their king, Nebuchadnezzar decided to select some of the children of Israel to serve in his palace. These individuals had to be good-looking and gifted in wisdom and knowledge. They were to be taught the language and literature of the Chaldeans. Daniel was one of four Jewish children selected to serve the king. In Daniel 2:1–13, we are told about the king's dreams and what he will do if his wise men could not interpret them for him:

> Now in the second year of Nebuchadnezzar's
> reign, Nebuchadnezzar had dreams; and his
> spirit was so troubled that his sleep left him.
> Then the king gave the command to call the
> magicians, the astrologers, the sorcerers, and
> the Chaldeans to tell the king his dreams. And
> the king said to them, "I have had a dream, and
> my spirit is anxious to know the dream." Then
> the Chaldeans spoke to the king in Aramaic,
> "O king, live forever! Tell your servants the
> dream, and we will give the interpretation." The
> king answered and said to the Chaldeans, "My
> decision is firm: If you do not make known the
> dream to me, and its interpretation, you shall
> be cut in pieces, and your houses shall be made
> an ash heap. "However, if you tell the dream
> and its interpretation, you shall receive from
> me gifts, rewards, and great honor. Therefore,
> tell me the dream and its interpretation." They
> answered again and said, "Let the king tell

his servants the dream, and we will give its interpretation." The king answered and said, "I know for certain that you would gain time, because you see that my decision is firm: "if you do not make known the dream to me, there is only one decree for you! For you have agreed to speak lying and corrupt words before me till the time has changed. Therefore tell me the dream, and I shall know that you can give me its interpretation." The Chaldeans answered the king, and said, "There is not a man on earth who can tell the king's matter; therefore no king, lord, or ruler has ever asked such things of any magician, astrologer, or Chaldean. "It is a difficult thing that the king requests, and there is no other who can tell it to the king except the gods, whose dwelling is not with flesh." For this reason the king was angry and very furious, and gave the command to destroy all the wise men of Babylon. So the degree went out, and they began killing the wise men; and they sought Daniel and his companions, to kill them.

Daniel subsequently meets with a man name Arioch, who was appointed by the king to kill the wise men. After Daniel persuades Arioch to let him meet with the king, he meets the king and then interprets Nebuchadnezzar's dream. Nebuchadnezzar's dream is perhaps the most famous one in the Bible. This dream is about a great statue. The head of the statue is of gold, the chest and arms are silver, the belly and thighs are bronze, the legs are iron, and the feet are partly iron and clay.

Daniel goes on to explain these different parts of the statue represent kingdoms. The current kingdom Babylon is the head of gold. After Babylon falls, the Medes and Persians come to power and are followed by the Greeks, which are followed by the Romans. Then in the last days, some form of the Roman Empire will be restored.

The final point of Nebuchadnezzar's dream is that God will restore his kingdom, which will never end and be perfect.

These dreams of Nebuchadnezzar were like the ones the Pharaoh of Egypt experienced. In both cases, the most powerful man in the world experienced disturbing dreams from God. Moreover, these rulers were not fearful men. Yet their spiritual dreams from God disturbed them greatly. Likewise, throughout the Bible when one received a dream from God, they knew it was supernatural. Although the ungodly may not have known their dreams were from God, they were powerful and compelled these men to search for answers.

Thus, God shows us in the Old Testament that spiritual dreams affect people. As a result, they change course.

In 1 Samuel 28:6, we are told about Saul's desperate attempt to hear from the Lord: "And when Saul inquired of the Lord, the Lord did not answer him, either by dreams or by Urim or by the prophets."

Backdrop

Although this passage is short, it reveals how vivid the Lord's dreams were to Saul. The Bible does not mention how often Saul received messages from God via dreams, but it was often enough that he trusted in them. Saul also depended on Samuel, a prophet who interceded on his behalf to the Lord. Samuel, though, had died by this time. Thus, without Samuel to reassure him and no dreams to ease his fears, Saul panicked because the Philistine Army was preparing to attack Israel.

Saul subsequently resorted to a desperate measure by seeking out a medium in the land. This was considered a great sin in the eyes of the Lord. Once he found a medium at Endor, he convinced her to conduct a séance. Before the woman conducted the ceremony, she asked Saul who he wanted to bring up. He wanted Samuel. Once the séance commenced, the woman saw a spirit that looked like an old man, and Saul perceived that it was Samuel. Although Samuel's appearance humbled Saul, he quickly became distraught after Samuel spoke these words in 1 Samuel 28:16–19:

Then Samuel said: "So why do you ask me,
seeing the Lord has departed from you and
has become your enemy? "And the Lord has
done for Himself as He spoke by me. For
the Lord has torn the kingdom out of your
hand and given it to your neighbor, David.
"Because you did not obey the voice of the Lord
nor execute His fierce wrath upon Amalek,
therefore the Lord has done this thing to you
this day. "Moreover the Lord will also deliver
Israel with you into the hand of the Philistines.
And tomorrow you and your sons will be
with me. The Lord will also deliver the army
of Israel into the hand of the Philistines."

Granted, Saul did not have the Holy Spirit living inside him,
which Christians have today. Instead, he had access to God through
prophets and dreams. So when his access to God was taken away
because of his disobedience, he felt lost and afraid. A spiritual dream
now would have comforted Saul because he knew it meant God
was with him. Without this assurance from God, fear consumed
Saul. This fear led him to desperate measures, which cost him his life.

In Job 33:14–16, we get some insight as to why God uses
dreams:

For God may speak in one way, or in
another, Yet man does not perceive it. In a
dream, in a vision of the night, When deep
sleep falls upon men, While slumbering
in their beds, Then He opens the ears
of men, And seals their instruction.

Backdrop

Throughout the book of Job, people expressed their opinions
about his suffering. In short, they implied Job was not being honest
about his spiritual condition. Thus, God is punishing him for

his disobedience. Likewise, Job insists he has done nothing wrong. Conversely, a younger man named Elihu contradicts what Job's friends are saying about the situation. Furthermore, Elihu disagrees with Job's assessment of the situation. Elihu contends that God is God. As such, he is all-powerful, fair, and worthy to be trusted, and no man can proclaim their righteousness before him.

The book of Job cites many Biblical principles that apply to us today. Although many pastors use the book of Job for sermons on suffering, there are other Biblical lessons in Job about God's will, purpose, and his mysterious ways. One of those mysterious ways is mentioned in Job 33:14–16. In short, these verses tell us that God reveals his will in different ways, and one of those ways is through dreams.

For our times, we can conclude from the book of Job that God has a plan. Although Job was never told why he had to suffer, in the end, he was blessed because he endured. As Christians, we too will experience hard times that conflict with our belief that God loves us. And when we do experience a period of suffering, God may not reveal the reasons why immediately. Because of this, we must be receptive to hear from God in unconventional ways, and one of those ways is through dreams.

In Matthew 1:20–21, The Angel of the Lord spoke to Joseph:

> But while he thought about these things,
> behold, an angel of the Lord appeared to
> him a dream, saying, "Joseph, son of David,
> do not be afraid to take to you Mary your
> wife, for that which is conceived in her is of
> the Holy Spirit. And she will bring forth a
> Son, and you shall call His name Jesus, for
> He will save His people from their sins."

Backdrop

Joseph by Jewish law was married to Mary. However, they were not allowed to be intimate until after the marriage ceremony. When Joseph found out that Mary was pregnant, he was distraught to say the least. But despite this perceived betrayal of trust by Mary, Joseph nevertheless pondered how to divorce Mary privately. No doubt Joseph loved Mary deeply, but it took a strong level of faith to accept what the Angel of the Lord told him. Likewise, there is no evidence in Scripture that Joseph was upset or tried to argue with the angel about the message.

This was the first spiritual dream recorded in the New Testament. And when you read Matthew 1:20–21, there is no indication that Joseph doubted or questioned whether this dream came from God. This dream convinced Joseph not to divorce Mary because any objections he had concerning Mary as his wife was not questioned anymore. I believe they were not raised anymore because Joseph knew from Old Testament stories that God spoke to people via dreams. So when he experienced his spiritual dream from the Angel of the Lord, he accepted it without question.

In Matthew 2:13–14, the Angel of the Lord spoke to Joseph again to flee to Egypt:

Now when they had departed, behold an angel of the Lord appeared to Joseph in a dream, saying, "Arise, take the young Child and His mother, flee to Egypt, and stay there until I bring you word; for Herod will seek the young Child to destroy Him." When he arose, he took the young child and his mother by night and departed for Egypt.

This was the second dream Joseph received from the Angel of the Lord. However, unlike the first dream, this one was a warning about a threat to his family along with instructions as to what to do. Joseph did not doubt this dream or its meaning. He immediately acted on it and headed to Egypt. So clearly, Joseph believed this dream without question. And like the first dream he received from God, this one was powerful, vivid, and etched in his memory.

The book of Matthew cites three dreams of Joseph. Although the Bible does not mention whether Joseph had other spiritual dreams, he probably had many more throughout his lifetime. The proof is in Scripture and based on how Joseph responded to the three dreams cited in the book of Matthew. In all three dreams, he obeyed the instructions given to him. So no doubt, when Joseph questioned his role as Jesus's earthly father, I believe his dreams from God reassured him.

This assurance from the Lord must have been powerful for Joseph because when Jesus was twelve, he separated from his family while they visited Jerusalem. After searching for Jesus for three days, they found him in the temple teaching. Jesus does not tell his mother that he is sorry. Instead, he simply tells her, "Don't you know that I must do my father's work?" That statement must have troubled Joseph greatly, but there is no mention in the Bible he became upset or bitter because of it. No doubt, Joseph was given insight into his role as Jesus's father. I believe one aspect of that insight was through dreams.

Joseph's third dream is recorded in Matthew 2:19–22:

> Now when Herod was dead, behold, an angel
> of the Lord appeared in a dream to Joseph in
> Egypt, saying, "Arise, take the young Child
> and His mother, and go to the land of Israel,
> for those who sought the young Child's life are
> dead." Then he arose, took the young Child and
> His mother, and came into the land of Israel.

There are two other dreams of note in the book of Matthew. The first one involved the Three Kings, who visited Jesus. It is recorded in Matthew 2:12: "Then, being divinely warned in a dream that they should not return to Herod, they departed for their own country another way."

Another cited dream concerned Pilate's wife. It is recorded in Matthew 27:19: "While he was sitting on the judgment seat, his wife sent to him, saying, 'Have nothing to do with that just Man, for I have suffered many things today in a dream because of Him.'" The Bible does not provide details of these dreams. Yet the Three Kings understood their dream to be a warning not to return to Herod. The dream of Pilate's wife remains a mystery though. Some have suggested in later years Pilate's wife became a Christian. The Catholic Church supports this position. In any event, she was disturbed by her dream.

The last dream cited in the New Testament is listed in Act 2:17: "And it shall come to pass in the last days, says God, That I will pour out of My Spirit all flesh; Your sons and your daughters shall prophesy, Your young men shall see visions, Your old men shall dream dreams."

This is the same passage as Joel 2:28–29. The last part of the passage is "Your old men shall dream dreams." The fact that old men shall have dreams is not surprising because spiritual dreams from God are filled with symbolism. And to interpret Biblical symbolism, you need to know your Bible. Furthermore, the dreams of Acts 2:17 refer to spiritual warfare and how to use the whole armor of God to fight against it.

Despite this, young people do experience spiritual dreams from God. Both Joseph of the Old and New Testament and Daniel received spiritual dreams when they were young men. Conversely, the dreams of Acts 2:17 will be a gift of the Holy Spirit that will be given to the church in the last days for spiritual warfare. Furthermore, the individuals who experience these spiritual dreams in the last days will be able to interpret them too. Given this, if you're experiencing spiritual dreams today, God may be preparing you for his work.

CHAPTER 5

Points to Remember

E ven though most Christians will experience spiritual dreams at some point in their lives, there is no Biblical principle that can predict when they will occur. On a personal note, God used dreams to open my eyes to spiritual warfare. In short, understanding how generational curses affected me and how Satan used them to hinder me. Likewise, I believe many Christians today are experiencing spiritual dreams because of generational curses within their family.

Since dreams are mysterious, you may not recognize a spiritual dream right away. Given this, even when a dream is filled with Biblical symbolism, and you're emotionally moved by it, you may still dismiss it. There are two reasons for this: First, your natural man (Sin Nature) will assume it's nothing supernatural. Instead, you will think it's just a weird dream. The second reason is because Satan will have you doubt the dream meant anything. Because if the dream was truly from God, Satan does not want you to understand it since many spiritual dreams are about him, and what he is doing to hinder you.

God reveals different messages through dreams based on your spiritual maturity. For example, many young adults or nonbelievers receive spiritual dreams conveying basic Christian principles. They may have dreams about swords, helmets, shields, and snakes. These are basic symbols that refer to God and Satan. For instance, the sword is God's Word, the helmet represents your thinking patterns, the shield represents God's protection, while snakes are always symbolic of Satan and his demons.

In contrast, mature believers will experience dreams that reveal hidden spiritual messages. These messages will reveal unknown Biblical principles the believer does not recognize. These Biblical principles could be generational curses, unconfessed sins of bitterness or unforgiveness, or some misunderstanding of Scripture. Unfortunately, many Christian denominations are ignoring established Biblical tenets to change with the times. Despite this, if God knows your spiritual potential and desire to serve him, he will open your eyes to false doctrines.

Expect Criticism

You can expect people to criticize your dreams, and there is nothing you can say or do to change their minds. Sadly, even pastors and strong believers will express doubts concerning your spiritual dreams. A lot of this criticism is based on their Christian experiences and doctrines. In short, they have never experienced a spiritual dream from God. Moreover, even if they had experienced spiritual dreams, they dismissed them.

When I first started to experience spiritual dreams, I was eager to share them with others. Also, I was hoping to get help in interpreting the meanings of these dreams. To my surprise, my pastors and other believers in my church were skeptical of my dreams. At the time, I attended a nondenominational church that believed in the Baptism of the Holy Spirit. Yet believing God would use dreams to convey messages to me seemed farfetched to them. So you can expect similar reactions from Christians in your church. Nevertheless, if you feel there is someone in your church who can help you understand your dreams, I will still encourage you to ask. Although your pastor may have attended seminary, his knowledge of Scripture is often denominational based. Therefore, his Biblical counsel to you on matters will reflect what he learned in seminary—not personal experiences. Granted, a pastor does not need to experience adultery, addiction, or unforgiveness to successfully counsel you on these issues. Conversely, if you're under spiritual attack or experiencing dreams, these types of situations call for personal experiences. Thus, sometimes seasoned Christians in your church can provide you better support.

Unpredictable

In many ways, spiritual dreams can enhance your faith because God is using dreams to show, warn, prepare, or strengthen you for his purposes. As a result, your faith will be strengthened after experiencing a spiritual dream from God; moreover, you can expect more spiritual dreams in the future. There is evidence of this throughout the Bible. For example, Daniel and Joseph of the Old and New Testaments received many spiritual dreams. In addition, even the ungodly such as King Nebuchadnezzar experienced more than one spiritual dream.

Although spiritual dreams are powerful, they don't replace a Christian's responsibility to pray, read Scripture, and be receptive to the inner voice of the Holy Spirit when difficulties arise. In many ways, spiritual dreams are like frosting on a cake: they just confirm what the Holy Spirit has told you. In addition, spiritual dreams add more details behind what the Holy Spirit told you. This is necessary because many churches today have lost their way. In short, they are spiritually dead. As a result, many Christians cannot discern the things of the Spirit.

Dreams and visions are gifts from God. So not every believer will experience them regularly. Yet God may convey an occasional dream to you to clarify something. Given this, do not get discouraged if other Christians you know experience spiritual dreams regularly—since you don't know God's purpose for conveying dreams to them. Furthermore, your spiritual maturity may be at a different level; therefore, you may not be ready to receive or interpret spiritual dreams.

If you start experiencing spiritual dreams frequently, don't expect them to continue. Although I've experienced numerous spiritual dreams over the years, I will sometimes go weeks or months between dreams. So even though God has given me this gift that I have used to warn and help others, they are unpredictable. In view of this, I've learned that spiritual dreams do not circumvent the inner voice of the Holy Spirit. In short, don't get enamored with the gift of spiritual dreams, but praise and thank God for the revelations you receive because of them.

As mentioned in previous chapters, you must understand Biblical symbolism to interpret your dreams. Some great resources for interpreting Biblical symbolism are study Bibles. So even if you're a new Christian, these study Bibles will help you interpret some of the symbols in your dreams. You will find common images in your dreams like sheep, lion, dragon, snake, wolves, helmet, and sword all refer to people, spiritual entities, or Scripture.

Scary Dreams

You will experience spiritual dreams that are scary. Despite this, God is not trying to scare you with these dreams. Instead, he is trying to warn you about an individual or situation. Most of these dark dreams refer to Satan and his demons, and what they are doing to hinder you spiritually. These dreams are necessary because most Christians don't understand demonic affliction. They don't understand demonic affliction because many churches do not teach on the subject. Pastors don't teach on the subject because many believers neither understand spiritual warfare nor are they interested in finding out more about it.

These dark dreams will unnerve you because of the fear effect. In short, you will wake up fearful. This fear is what nonbelievers experience when Satan attacks them. Many Christians will never feel this fear, chiefly because God's hedge of protection is around them. Also, an immature believer may abandon their faith if they think this fear is associated with Christianity. Given this, if you experience a series of dark dreams, God knows your spiritual maturity. Likewise, God wants you to address the demonic strongholds in your life.

Remember, to interpret the meaning of any spiritual dream, you must know Biblical symbolism. Dark dreams are no different. The only difference is the symbolism within dark dreams. Some common symbolism within dark dreams are snakes, dark shadows, swords, helmets, and shields. These basic symbols are not difficult to interpret. What is difficult to interpret are the messages for these symbols. For example, snakes represent Satan or his demons. Therefore, your job is to discern why you're under spiritual attack.

Another aspect of dark dreams involves revelations concerning people you love or respect. Sadly, these dreams are revealing spiritual facts about people of deception. In short, they are wolves among sheep. Many times, these individuals are not truly saved. Unfortunately, many churches have members who are not saved. Also, many of these unsaved individuals are in positions of authority in churches. Your job is not to expose them, but to use discernment when interacting with them.

Even though dark dreams can be disconcerting, you should not dread these dreams. Instead, thank God for his revelations. You must always remember there are reasons God is revealing things to you via dreams—even if the dreams are scary. On a personal note, it took months before I understood how to interpret spiritual dreams. Because of this, sometimes you may have to wait on the Lord for the interpretation of a dream.

CHAPTER 6

Spiritual Warfare

God uses spiritual dreams for many purposes. One of those purposes concerns the hidden world of spiritual warfare. This is a subject that few pastors on television, the radio, or in churches want to address. Since it's a topic that is disconcerting and one that believers prefer to ignore. Likewise, Christian denominations are divided over issues of gay marriage, homosexuality, and female pastors. As a result, the church is divided and cannot agree on measures for tackling spiritual warfare throughout the world.

Another factor to weigh about spiritual warfare is the vast amount of information available through the Internet. There is conflicting information on every subject—especially religious beliefs. As a result, many people feel intimidated if they support traditional Biblical principles. Also, something as controversial as spiritual warfare with Satan and his demons seems far-fetched to many people—even Christians.

This explosion of information coupled with society's apathy toward Christianity has changed how people view God—especially the young. I observed this firsthand while working as a counselor with service members who served in Iraq or Afghanistan. Many of these service members had physical and mental disabilities due to their deployments. Sadly, many of these individuals had no religious upbringing or faith in God. I found this perplexing since many of them had experienced the horrors of war.

Based on my experience working with service members, I know there is a spiritual void among young adults. Because of this, God is using dreams to draw young people to him. Although it's the job of the Holy Spirit to draw people to Jesus, many young people cannot discern the urges of the Holy Spirit because they don't have Christian upbringings. As a result, they don't know how to repent and accept Christ as savior. I often hear this from family members involved in ministry. Moreover, I often get requests from them to help interpret disturbing dreams about people they minister to. Many of their dreams concern spiritual warfare.

Spiritual Warfare

The main purpose of spiritual warfare is to prevent Christians from growing spiritually. Satan will do whatever he can to steal, kill, or destroy a person. Yes, the devil is out to get you. However, once you're saved, his plan of attack against you changes. Satan's new strategy is to frustrate you to the point your life does not produce fruit or works for Christ. This is what spiritual warfare entails.

Spiritual warfare is Satan's attempt to keep the body of Christ from doing its work. Satan plans his attacks against you depending on your spiritual strengths and weaknesses. Although only God knows your thoughts, Satan can determine your intentions based on how you speak, act, and live. Unfortunately, many Christians realize their lifestyle conflicts with their faith, but they are not concerned enough about it to change how they live. As a result, Satan has no reason to attack them because they pose no threat to him. Conversely, when one tries to change their lifestyle and start living the Christian life, they will experience spiritual attacks.

When Satan attacks you because of your testimony for Christ, you cannot fight him physically or emotionally because Satan is a spirit, so he must be fought with weapons of the spirit. In Ephesians 6:12, we are told about our enemy: "For we do not wrestle against flesh and blood, but against principalities, against powers, against the rulers of the darkness of this age, against spiritual hosts of wickedness in the heavenly places."

Why Evil

Few would dispute there is evil in the world. The only disagreement is why there is evil in the world. Sociologists contend people are simply a by-product of their culture. So if they do evil acts that are acceptable within their culture, they are not evil. Conversely, they contend different cultures have no right to judge other ones that practice different values and religious beliefs. In short, no one is right nor wrong, but a by-product of their culture.

The argument against this premise is that many people reject their cultural values and beliefs. If people reject their cultural norms, then what controls their behavior? If it's based on free will, then why do some people behave responsibly while others are irresponsible? If individuality or free will determines how one acts within a culture, then why would a person choose to reject acceptable behavior when there are negative consequences for doing so? This seems to conflict with the theory that we evolved because of our superior intelligence. Granted, our technology has evolved, but mankind's behavior has not.

Sociologists have conducted many research studies about the moral beliefs of primitive cultures. These studies often show primitive cultures share common moral beliefs as those in Western countries. For example, acts of stealing, murder, coveting, false witness, adultery, or disrespect for parents were always considered wrong things to do within cultures. Even within cultures where traditional religious beliefs are not taught, people have a sense of what is right and wrong. This moral paradigm can be observed among children with no religious upbringing too. So clearly, human beings have been imprinted with something at birth that provides them with a moral compass. Therefore, if we are born with a moral compass or soul, do we concede that God is responsible for it?

If mankind was created with a moral compass or soul, then why do so many people reject the religious tenets of their culture? For example, 70 percent of Americans consider themselves Christians, but many of them do not attend church often nor do they practice the moral teachings of the faith. Given this, are these individuals Christians? If not, what are the factors that prove that one is a Christian?

Most theologians would agree Christians believe Jesus Christ was the Son of God, who died for their sins. Likewise, because of Jesus, mankind's relationship with God the Father was restored. A relationship that was severed because of Adam's original sin in the Garden. Although there are many Christian denominations in the world, the belief that Jesus was the Son of God unites all believers.

Satan

There are two other principles of Christianity that most theologians agree on: our soul never dies, and we have free will. The Bible seems to imply angels and demons are immortal too, and they have free will. This is important because it provides an explanation for evil in the world. Evil is not a feeling, but a negative force that is afflicting mankind. The Bible is clear there is evil in the world because of Satan and his demons. Satan is called the Adversary because he torments mankind and prevents Christians from doing good works. If true, then why did God create a devil?

In the book of Revelation, we are told about Satan's punishment for defying God:

> And war broke out in heaven: Michael and his
> angels fought with the dragon; and the dragon
> and his angels fought, but they did not prevail,
> nor was a place found for them in heaven any
> longer. So the great dragon was cast out, that
> serpent of old, called the Devil and Satan, who
> deceives the whole world; he was cast to the
> earth and his angels were cast out with him.
> (Rev. 12:7–9)

These verses clearly outline the devil's fate and the consequences for mankind because of it.

God did not create a devil. He created an archangel name Lucifer. His fall from heaven was due to his disobedience. Satan's coup in heaven occurred because he believed his power rivaled that of God's—even though God created him. And clearly, he had unique powers and gifts other angels believed in. This was evident because one-third of the angels in heaven followed him. I think many theologians have underestimated how powerful and gifted Satan was in heaven.

Satan still has power today, which he uses to attack mankind and cause bad things to happen in the world. His main weapons are demonic persuasion and temptation. Satan uses these weapons to attack our minds with negative thoughts. Despite this, people have free will to reject or accept his evil thoughts. Therefore, for a demonic thought to take hold, a person must agree with it, and act on it. Even original sin by Adam and Eve was an agreement to do what Satan suggested.

Sadly, one of the consequences for mankind because of original sin was forfeiting control of the earth to Satan. We find many verses in the New Testament to support this claim. For example, in the book of Matthew, there is an interplay between Jesus and the devil. We find this in Matthew 4:8–10:

> Again, the devil took Him up on an exceedingly
> high mountain, and Showed Him all the
> kingdoms of the world and their glory. And
> he said to Him, "All these things I will give
> You if You will fall down and worship me."
> Then Jesus said to him, "Away with you, Satan!
> For it is written, You shall worship the Lord
> your God, and Him only you shall serve."

Clearly, these verses state that Satan has the authority to influence the affairs of mankind. Furthermore, it provides us insight for understanding why there is evil in the world.

Many Christians believe Satan was defeated when Jesus Christ died on the cross for our sins. Thus, his authority to attack and torment Christians ended two thousand years ago. The Bible seems to support this position. Still, a Christian must live a life that honors

71

God if they want his hedge of protection from the attacks of Satan and his demons. We find in 1 Peter 5:8–9 confirmation of this: "Be sober, be vigilant; because your adversary the devil walks about like a roaring lion, seeking whom he may devour." Peter is not talking to nonbelievers. He is talking to Christians. Therefore, Christians must keep their focus on Jesus Christ by living lives that honor God. If not, there are negative spiritual consequences.

Even people of faith struggle with thinking patterns that are considered sinful. For example, feelings of anger, hate, bitterness, lust, envy, pride, unforgiveness, and covetousness will destroy a Christian's testimony for Christ. And once Christians lose their testimony for Christ due to bad behavior or thinking patterns, they open the door for Satan. Furthermore, God is not obligated to keep his hedge of protection around Christians who won't confess their sins. This is outlined in John 10:10: "The thief does not come except to steal, and to kill, and to destroy. I have come that they may have life, and that they may have it more abundantly."

Whole Armor

Given this powerful warning concerning Satan, how can anyone fight off these dark thoughts and avoid bad behaviors that will destroy their testimony for Christ? The Bible provides us an answer in Ephesians 6:10–18:

> Finally, my brethren, be strong in the Lord and
> in the power of his might. Put on the whole
> armor of God, that you may be able to stand
> against the wiles of the devil. For we do not
> wrestle against flesh and blood, but against
> principalities, against powers, against rulers of
> the darkness of this age, against spiritual hosts
> of wickedness in the heavenly places. Therefore
> take up the whole armor of God, that you
> may be able to withstand in the evil day, and
> having done all, to stand. Stand therefore,
> having girded your waist with truth, having

put on the breast plate of righteousness, and
having shod your feet with the preparation of
the gospel of peace; above all, taking the shield
of faith with which you will be able to quench
all the fiery darts of the wicked one. And take
the helmet of salvation, and the sword of the
Spirit, which is the word of God; praying
always with all prayer and supplication in
the Spirit, being watchful to this end with all
perseverance and supplication for all saints.

These verses outline all the evil forces against Christians and
the means to confront them. Still, one must discern the symbolic
language used in these verses. For instance, putting on the whole
armor of God is a metaphor for three spiritual weapons Christians
need to confront Satan and his demons: the helmet, shield, and sword.

The helmet is symbolic for controlling your thoughts. Satan's
greatest weapon is deception through our thoughts. Thus, bad
thinking will produce bad results. Our main protection against these
attacks from Satan is God. This is what the shield represents. To
fight the enemy, we use the sword. The sword is symbolic of the
Word of God. In short, you cite Scripture when dark thoughts or
situations arise.

The whole armor of God is not difficult to understand;
however, applying it to your life is difficult. It is difficult because you
must fight your flesh—your human nature, the world, and Satan.
The battle to defeat these three impediments is not a physical fight,
but one of the mind. So one must believe God is their strength,
and through faith in him, one can overcome any obstacle. Because
we are what we think, we think what we are. In short, you must
have fanatical faith in God to fight off the attacks of Satan and
his demons. This can only be achieved by knowing God—not by
knowing about him. You know God through prayer and meditation,
by reading your Bible often, and by listening to the inner voice of
the Holy Spirit.

The next component of the whole armor of God is the helmet.
The helmet is a reference for controlling what you see and think.
Hence, what you watch on television, the music you listen to, and

people you interact with all affect how you think. And if all these activities along with the people you associate with belittle or ignore the things of God, you'll be vulnerable to attacks from the enemy. That is the message of Ephesians 6:10–18.

To get your mind to think correctly and holy, you must put information into it that points toward God. No, you don't abandon all your friends and family, but you need to change what you watch on television, listen to on the radio, and the people you want to be around. Also, you must be involved with a church and read your Bible often. These changes are just the first steps. The hard part is allowing the Holy Spirit to take control of your life. This cannot occur until you are willing to change how you think, act, and believe.

The last component of the whole armor of God is the sword. The sword refers to knowing Scripture or your Bible. In practical terms, it's knowing what the Bible says about a given situation. For example, you're feeling tired and defeated a b o u t a situation or person. A verse for this situation would be "I can do all things through Christ who strengthens me." By citing God's Word instead of resorting to the things of the world, you are expressing faith in God. Remember, God is only obligated to intervene for a person who expresses faith in him. However, it takes time and experience to develop faith in Scripture when things go wrong. Hence, the same mentality one needs to prepare for a marathon applies to faith in Scripture too. In short, you must apply Biblical principles to your daily routine.

Even after a Christian learns how to apply the whole armor of God, they are not exempt from demonic attacks. We find confirmation of this in 2 Corinthians 12:7: "And lest I should be exalted above measure by the abundance of the revelations, a thorn in the flesh was given to me, a messenger of Satan to buffet me, lest I be exalted above measure." This is Paul talking to the Corinthians about his suffering for the cause of Christ. Although Paul did nothing worthy of torment by this demon, God allowed it to keep him humbled. Even though Paul was perhaps the greatest Christian who ever lived, he still had to keep his natural man (sin nature) in check by relying on God. Hence, this tormenting spirit kept Paul grounded and focused on Jesus Christ.

The main point of 2 Corinthians 12:7 is that God allowed Paul to be tormented by this demon. We don't know how Paul was tormented, but clearly, it bothered him. This is confirmed in 2 Corinthians 12:8–9:

> Concerning this thing I pleaded with the Lord
> three times that it might depart from me.
> And He said to me, "My grace is sufficient
> for you, for My strength is made perfect in
> weakness." Even though no man suffered more
> than Paul for the cause of Christ, God still
> refused to cast off this tormenting spirit. Paul
> knew why: lest I be exalted above measure.

Paul understood that sometimes suffering is necessary to keep us grounded. Many Christians today refuse to believe that God sometimes allows suffering for his purposes.

Church Views

The Church today has three views concerning Satan. The first view is that Satan was defeated two thousand years ago. So Christians have nothing to fear from Satan and his demons because he was defeated when Christ died on the cross. The second view is that Satan is a roaring lion ready to pounce on you. Thus, any sinful activity can instantly cause a demonic attack. The last view contends that Satan never existed. Instead, he was created during the Dark Ages to keep people fearful and loyal to the Church. Many nonbelievers share this view today. Sadly, many Christians doubt the existence of a literal devil too.

If the devil is not real, then why did Jesus Christ die on the cross for our sins? The answer was to restore our relationship with God because of original sin by Adam and Eve. Satan caused mankind's separation from God when he deceived Eve into eating the forbidden fruit in the Garden. Given this, one cannot claim to be a Christian and doubt the existence of Satan. Because since the

Fall, mankind has been thrown into a spiritual war between Good versus Evil. This is a war for the souls of mankind. Unfortunately, many Christians do not understand this war. As a result, Satan and his demons are ruling the earth with an iron fist. Hence, the spiritual condition of the world won't change until Christians exercise their authority over Satan in Jesus's name.

If mankind is locked in a spiritual war between the forces of Good versus Evil, then why aren't pastors preaching on this subject to their congregations? There are three possible reasons: First, pastors are scared to lose their ministries because this message is not popular or uplifting. Second, many churches today have lukewarm Christians who lack faith in Christ and the authority of Scripture. Thus, they cannot accept or discern deep spiritual issues. The third reason is outlined in 2 Corinthians 11:13–15. These verses warn about false teachers:

> For much are false apostles, deceitful workers,
> transforming themselves into apostles of Christ.
> And no wonder! For Satan himself transforms
> himself into an angel of light. Therefore it is
> no great thing if his ministers also transform
> themselves into ministers of righteousness,
> whose end will be according to their works.

Most Christian churches today are pastored by men and women who believe Jesus Christ is the Son of God. So I don't believe the warning in 2 Corinthians 11:13–15 applies to most pastors today. However, some Christian ministers are deceiving their congregations. Sadly, the main culprit for the decline of Christianity in the United States is our culture. Likewise, because Christians won't reject the secular messages of our culture, this has weakened the church. Because of this, Satan has the church in disarray while he is causing havoc throughout the world.

Bad Consequences

Many factors are responsible for why bad things happen to good people. The main reason is Satan and his demons. Yes, Satan is a powerful factor that can be blamed for many of the bad things in the world. However, there are different aspects or factors associated with Satan.

The first Satan factor is God does not protect nonbelievers. Our opinion of who is considered good does not matter to God. Because if one is not born again, they are not justified before God. In Matthew 19:17, Jesus confirms this: "So He said to him, 'Why do you call Me good? No one is good but One, that is, God. But if you want to enter into life, keep the commandments.'"

Another Satan factor concerns Christians who openly sin and don't forgive. Although a Christian's spirit is b o r n   a g a i n, their soul is not. The soul is our thoughts, emotions, and will. Thus, all Christians must be vigilant to keep their soul and spirit lined up. This cannot be done through human efforts. Instead, it must be done by submitting to the urges of the Holy Spirit that resides in every Christian's heart. When Christians ignore or refuse to listen to the Holy Spirit, they start a process of disengagement with God. Furthermore, when they engage in sinful activities that destroy their testimony for Christ, they subsequently trigger spiritual consequences. Although a single sinful act may not trigger these spiritual consequences, a refusal to repent of it will.

There are many stories in the Bible about men of faith who fell out of fellowship with God because of sin. Many of these men repented and turned back to God; however, some never repented and died because of their disobedience. Christians too can engage in sinful activities that will break their fellowship with God. As a result, they open themselves up to demonic attacks. For example, excessive drinking or drug use will destroy a Christian's testimony for Christ; moreover, they could lose their life because of it. Likewise, hidden sins such as pornography, gambling, unforgiveness, and bitterness will demoralize Christians, and they will lose their faith in God too. These hidden sins can also generate feelings of hopelessness and doubts about one's salvation. Unfortunately, some Christians even succumb to suicide because of despair.

When Christians fall out of fellowship with God, they are vulnerable to attacks from Satan. Although Satan cannot read your mind, he can discern patterns of behavior that provide him opportunities to attack you. We get warnings of this in 1 Peter 5:8 and in the book of Job. No, Satan is not everywhere, but he has many demons. These demons have areas of responsibility and individuals to watch over. So Christians need to keep alert for the snares of the enemy.

As noted, a Christian's spirit is born again, but their soul is not. The soul wars against the inner voice of the Holy Spirit. So if an unconfessed sin becomes ingrained in a Christian's soul, Satan gains control. Once Satan has control, bad things can happen. Although God is love, he cannot allow Christians to sin with impunity. In view of this, God's hedge of protection from Satan can be lifted from Christians when they fail to repent of known sins.

Many Christians and nonbelievers know negative results can occur when people do bad things. Yet often, they want to blame someone for it. As a result, when loved ones or friends suffer because of bad choices, Christians may cite Satan as the culprit. While nonbelievers may claim karma as the reason for their fate. Conversely, it's hard for Christians to accept that people who live for the Lord will suffer. For instance, the tragic loss of a child or spouse without warning can shake even the strongest person of faith. Likewise, a terminal medical diagnosis of self can invoke fear and anger that God cannot be trusted.

Although Christians know Satan is responsible for many of the bad things that happen in the world directly or indirectly—indirectly due to original sin by mankind. It is still hard for believers to accept that God allows Satan to attack his children for no apparent reason. Still, although it's frustrating, like Job of the Old Testament, sometimes Christians suffer in the world for unknown reasons.

CHAPTER 7

Loneliness

Since dreams are personal, God uses them to convey messages about spiritual scars. Even though a Christian's spirit is born again, their soul is not. Because of this, Christians cannot harbor unforgiveness or bitterness toward others. If they do so, bitter roots can form and affect their relationship with God and others. This spiritual tenet is one of the main reasons many Christians never mature. This is outlined in Hebrews 12:15: "Looking carefully lest anyone fall short of the grace of God; lest any root of bitterness springing up cause trouble, and by this many become defiled."

All people need intimate relationships with others and God. Often the world is shocked when a beautiful woman or famous man commits suicide. Many often blame drugs or mental health problems for the suicides of famous people.

Despite this belief, the frequency of famous people committing suicide suggests these individuals felt alone and trapped by their despair. Even though these famous people had millions of fans and an entourage of people handling their affairs, yet they felt alone and decided to end their lives.

The elderly experience loneliness too as they age and are placed in care facilities. Although adult children had good intentions for placing aging parents into homes, they often have busy lives that keep them from visiting loved ones often. As a result, close family relationships deteriorate over time. This sense of abandonment by family members often causes depression and loneliness among the elderly. Sadly, these negative feelings play a major role in the higher suicide rates among the elderly.

Chronic loneliness also affects young adults and teens. Although many lonely adults and teens have family members and friends they interact with daily, these relationships are not intimate. Because true intimate relationships involve people you trust, feel comfortable around, and love you unconditionally. Most people view their mothers in this way. Sadly, if one's mother was not a supporting loving presence for them, their level of trust and compassion for others will be affected too.

No doubt, intimate relationships are crucial for one's mental, physical, and spiritual health. Because of this, if one feels isolated and unloved, acute loneliness will follow. People have an innate desire to be loved and involved with others. The Bible seems to support this contention too. We find in Genesis 2:18 God's confirmation that one should not be alone: "And the Lord God said, 'It is not good that man should be alone; I will make him a helper comparable to him.'"

In Genesis 2:24, we are then told about the marital covenant and why people today desperately want this type of relationship: "Therefore a man shall leave his father and mother and be joined to his wife, and they shall become one flesh." Throughout history, people have sought this type of love. Unfortunately, many have pursued this type of love regardless of the cost to themselves and others.

Relationships

The most important relationships children have before entering middle school are with their parents. Thereafter, the relationships they form with peers in middle school and high school shapes their identity. As a result, the teen years either reinforce their self-confidence or demoralizes it. For instance, boys who excel in athletics or academics always get recognition from peers. Whereas boys who are neither good athletes nor students get little recognition from peers. Conversely, teenage girls' value physical attractiveness and their popularity among peers. Although academics are important to girls too, it's not how they compare themselves to peers. Also, girls desire relationships with boys. Unlike boys, though, these relationshipsare not driven by physical desires, but a desire for emotional closeness. Given this, girls who struggle with boy relationships in high school can develop low self-esteem; moreover, a bad dating event can scar a girl emotionally.

Unfortunately, teenage girls who have bad experiences with boys can be affected emotionally. There is a powerful verse in the Bible that confirms wounds of the heart can affect us. We find this in Proverbs 23:7: "For as he thinks inhis heart, so is he. 'Eat and drink!' he says to you, But his heart is not with you."

The recent Supreme Court confirmation hearings demonstrated the effects of emotional wounds. The focus of these hearings concerned an alleged sexual assault by the nominee while in high school. Yet the testimonies of the two parties conveyed different realities and whether the event occurred. For example, the judge had no memory of the assault. So he kept citing his athletic and academic successes in high school and college to the senators. Furthermore, he cited his stellar record as a lawyer and judge. His point was clear: a person with such impeccable academic credentials and career successes should be trusted. Therefore, he could not have committed the alleged assault.

In contrast, the woman's testimony emphasized the event and how it affected her life. Although she achieved academic and career successes too, these accomplishments did not override her emotional pain from the alleged assault. Further, her senate testimony about the incident was powerful and moving. Even though her testimony was not proof the nominee committed the alleged assault, she believed he did. Thus, no doubt, the emotional scars from this event had a lifelong effect.

Many women across the country empathized with her plight. As a result, this rekindled the "Me Too Movement" of 2017. And no doubt, this confirmation hearing played a role in the election results of 2018. Although some would argue this accusation against the Supreme Court nominee was politically motivated, the testimony from the accuser opened wounds for many women. Therefore, whether one is a Republican or Democrat, the issue of sexual assault in our society was brought to light. Likewise, those who have experienced a sexual assault are forever changed by it.

Effects

There are many negative effects after one has experienced emotional wounds. The main effect for women concerns future relationships with men. A woman who has been emotionally wounded or sexually assaulted by a man will have intimacy and trust issues. Likewise, they often withdraw from family members too. Given this, a wounded individual must release their hurts. Although this is the solution for emotional healing, the process of getting there may take years.

Women are communicators, and they need to express their hurts in words. So whether one pursues a secular or Christian counselor, they must address all three components of self: the physical, emotional, and spiritual components. Although physical scars from past wounds can heal in time, emotional and spiritual scars are difficult to heal and release.

Given this, to release these scars, one must stop thinking about them, have no anxiety or fear because of them, and forgive the individuals who caused them. Although this is the solution for emotional and spiritual healing, the steps to get there can be elusive.

Although emotionally wounded individuals will seek counseling, a secular counselor cannot address a wounded soul. Instead, they only address the psychological reasons for one's pain and offer techniques for coping with it. Also, they will prescribe medication to address any anxiety or depression associated with one's pain. This is the standard operating procedure for secular counselors; however, this treatment plan does not address the scars of a wounded soul.

The dictionary definition of a soul is "the spiritual or immaterial part of a human being regarded as immortal." This definition is vague, to say the least. Many theologians believe one's soul is their thoughts, emotions, and will. In short, what governs a person's behavior and beliefs? Most would agree this is a better definition of one's soul. Therefore, how does one heal a wounded soul? Conversely, can psychological counseling and medication heal all the components of a wounded soul? If not, then how can people with wounded souls be healed?

A person with a wounded soul must be healed by God. Yet if a person won't admit they have wounds, God won't override their will. The Bible is clear about matters about God's attention: ask, knock, and seek; moreover, one must repent of known or hidden sin. Therefore, if one refuses to forgive the parties responsible for their wounded soul, this is unforgiveness. So the first step in this process is to acknowledge these wounds and must forgive the individuals who caused them. This cannot be done by the natural man (our sin nature). Instead, this must be done by the spiritual man empowered by the Holy Spirit.

Holy Spirit

Most Christians do not understand the role of the Holy Spirit. Even though the Holy Spirit is often cited during sermons, many believers have never felt his presence. Granted, if one is truly saved, they were convicted of their sins by the Holy Spirit. Thereafter, a believer must learn to discern the voice of the Holy Spirit. Although a believer has access to the Holy Spirit if they are truly born- again, many factors can block his presence in one's life. One of these factors is the church you attend.

The church is divided on many issues to include the role of the Holy Spirit. Although all Christian denominations believe in the Holy Spirit, what is taught about him varies within churches. Granted, most denominations believe the Holy Spirit is part of the Trinity, but they disagree on his purpose and whether he is a separate individual.

This confusion about the Holy Spirit is due to denominational bias. Many church services today are conducted more like programmed events than as a time to worship God as one body. Sadly, these types of church services block the Holy Spirit from revealing himself to believers.

These secular worship services have also played a major role in declining church attendance for Catholics and mainstream Protestants. Conversely, Charismatic churches have grown steadily; moreover, most adults who are coming to Christ today are joining these types of churches. The reason: these churches emphasize the gifts of the Holy Spirit and the importance of listening to his inner voice.

We find in Luke 24:49 Scripture to support the power and importance of the Holy Spirit: "Behold, I send the Promise of My Father upon you; but tarry in the city of Jerusalem until you are endued with power from on high." This verse confirms the power Christians have in the world because of the Holy Spirit. Likewise, this verse stresses the importance of waiting on the Holy Spirit before embarking on God's work.

Although Christians must learn to listen to the Holy Spirit, many believers have never been taught how to do it. Instead, they have been told to proclaim the sinner's prayer, pray, read their Bibles, and attend church services. Yet these actions alone won't draw a person closer to God. Granted, these actions may strengthen one's religious convictions and faith, but without the Holy Spirit, there can be no intimate relationship with God the Father. Since it's the Holy Spirit that reveals the things of God to us.

This is important because all Christians will experience storms in life. The only question is how we respond to these storms. Yes, praying, reading your Bible, and church attendance can strengthen you during difficult times. However, doing these religious activities without the presence of the Holy Spirit won't comfort you. Sadly, thousands of Christians have left the church because they were hurt by the comments of other believers. Likewise, these hurt Christians are mad at God for allowing their misfortunes to occur.

Many Christians harbor anger toward believers and God because they don't understand their two natures: spiritual and carnal. Our spiritual nature determines how we worship and obey God. Our carnal nature is how sin controls what we think, do, and say. Thus, when one accepts Christ, their spiritual nature changes, but they still war against the carnal man. This is a lifelong process that is difficult. Unfortunately, this war between our two natures causes a lot of confusion and disappointments among Christians.

This war between our two natures is not a personal view, but one based on Scripture. The strongest argument for this position can be found in the book of Romans. In Romans 7:14–25, we get Paul's dissertation of our two natures:

> For we know that the law is spiritual, but I am carnal sold under sin. For what I am doing, I do not understand. For what I will to do, that I do not practice; but what I hate, that I do. If, then, I do what I will not to do, I agree with the law that it is good. But now, it is no longer I who do it, but sin that dwells in me. For I know that in me that is, in my flesh nothing good dwells, for to will is present with me, but how to perform what is good I do not find. For the good that I will to do, I do not do; but the evil I will not to do, that I practice. Now if I do what I will not to do, it is no longer I who do it, but sin that dwells in me. I find then a law, that evil is present with me, the one who wills to do good. For I delight in the law of God according to the inward man. But I see another law in my members warring against the law of my mind, and bringing me into captivity to the law of sin which is in my members. O wretched man that I am! Who will deliver me from this body of death? I thank God—through Jesus Christ our Lord! So then, with the mind I myself serve the law of God, but with the flesh the law of sin.

Many theologians contend Paul was the greatest Christian who ever lived. Few would dispute the merits of this contention. Yet the man who saw heaven says the things he hates, he does. Furthermore, Paul describes the mental, physical, and spiritual forces that affect him and us daily. In short, there is an inner battle within us between our spirit and flesh. This battle to live godly cannot be won with our will. Instead, we must listen to the inner voice of the Holy Spirit and allow Him to guide our actions daily.

To yield to the Holy Spirit, one must learn to trust God without question. This is not an easy process. Instead, it's a gradual process that occurs after one has experienced many failures and disappointments in life. Because in many ways, we need to be broken to the extent that our hope and faith is in God alone. Unfortunately, the gifted individuals in our society are harder to break spiritually since the world, flesh, and Satan tells them they are intelligent and resourceful. Thus, they don't need to ask or wait on God for help. We get confirmation of this in James 2:5: "Hearken, my beloved, Has not God chosen the poor of this world rich in faith, and heirs of the kingdom which he has promised to them that love him?"

On a personal note, I have been a Christian for over forty years. Sadly, I had to experience many hardships before I learned to yield to the Holy Spirit. This reliance on the Holy Spirit did not occur overnight. Instead, it occurred steadily as I trusted God more and more; however, I had to keep my self-reliance at bay. Although people and the world often reward self-reliance, God cannot use a person who won't rely on him.

In view of this, although I have been frustrated and disillusioned through the years, I have learned to trust God to guide me daily. This is a decision all believers must make to fulfill God's plan for their life. So whether one is a Christian or not, God has given everyone spiritual strengths and weaknesses. So in a perfect world, everybody will reach their full spiritual potential and achieve great things for God.

Unfortunately, the Bible is clear that few will inherit eternal life—much less fulfill God's plan for their life. In view of this, if you're a Christian, you're already blessed and highly favored! Since most people in the world don't know Christ, nor do they have a desire to know him because they don't have the gift of the Holy Spirit. Thus, it's a gift from God that allowed you to accept Christ. Once you understand that accepting Christ is a gift from God, your outlook concerning past failures and hurts won't consume you anymore. The key, though, is learning to yield to the Holy Spirit.

There is no ten-point plan that will increase your reliance on the Holy Spirit. Despite this, all true believers have the Holy Spirit residing inside them. Still, the impediment that keeps you from enjoying his presence is sin. In short, you must release hurts, anger, bitterness, and strongholds that keep you in spiritual bondage. Spiritual bondage is something from your past that controls how you think, act, and believe about a situation or person. Many times, believers won't admit they have issues against anyone or God, but they do. So the first step is to confess these things to God and release them.

If you sincerely petition God to remove all spiritual scars from your soul, he must respond. Because of this, if the pain from past wounds remains, ask God for discernment because there must be other spiritual wounds you don't realize-- such as generational curses and judgments within your bloodline. Thus, you have the authority in Jesus's name to remove these generational curses. Do not doubt this authority or God's power to deliver you from anything! Also, always remember that Satan wants to keep you in spiritual bondage. So reject his negative thoughts of doubt and discouragement.

Once Christians truly surrender to the Holy Spirit and God, they will not suffer acute loneliness. Granted, they may want company or even physical touch, but they will not experience loneliness that consumes them. Because they are not alone. Instead, they have three intimate relationships that can fulfill every need.

Those relationships are with God the Father, God the Holy Spirit, and God the Son. Every Christian who wants this relationship with the Trinity can have it. God is not a respecter of persons. Therefore, if one wants to experience the presence of God that will move them to tears, they must ask, knock, and seek it.

Salvation Verses

For God so loved the world that He gave His
only begotten Son, that whoever believes in Him
should not perish but have everlasting life.
(John 3:16)

That if you confess with mouth the Lord Jesus and believe
in your heart that God has raised Him from the dead, you
will be saved. For with the heart one believes unto righteous,
and with the mouth confession is made unto salvation.
(Rom. 10:9–10)

For the wages of sin is death, but the gift of God
is eternal life in Christ Jesus our Lord.
(Rom. 6:23)

Jesus answered and said to him, "Most assuredly, I say to you,
unless one is born again, he cannot see the kingdom of God."
(John 3:3)

Not everyone who says to Me, "Lord, Lord,"
shall enter the kingdom of heaven, but he who
does the will of My Father in heaven.
(Matt. 7:21)

I am the door. If anyone enters by Me, he will be
saved, and will go in and out and find pasture.
(John 10:9)

Jesus said to him, "I am the way, the truth, and the 1life.
No one comes to the Father except through Me."
(John 14:6)

Scripture

Every Christian has their favorite verses they dwell on during difficult times. Further, it's not necessary to cite Scripture verbatim since God knows the intent and faith we have in his Word. Given this, here are some Scripture segments to cite during difficult times:

1. I can do all things through Christ who strengthens me.
2. If God is for you, who can be against you.
3. Resist the devil, and he will flee from you.
4. Greater is he who is in me, than he who is in the world.
5. We cannot even imagine the love God has for those that love him.
6. Every thought is captive, every spirit is tested.
7. Seek first the kingdom of God, and all these things will be added.
8. No good thing will God withhold from those who love him.
9. If I am obedient, I will eat the fruit of the lamb.
10. The steps of a righteous man are ordered by God.
11. The Lord will never allow the righteous man to stumble.
12. When I am weak, then I am strong.
13. It is not I that live, but Christ who lives in me.
14. We cannot even imagine the blessings of those that love and fear the Lord.
15. Nothing formed against me can stand.
16. There is a season for all things.
17. I do not have a spirit of fear, but of power, love, and sound mind.
18. If you draw closer to me, I will draw closer to you.

Other Books Written by Frank Angerillo

Satan's Evil Scheme

Many people question if Satan is real and whether he is responsible for evil in the world, even though the Bible is clear that Satan exists and influences world events. Despite this, pastors are reluctant to preach sermons about Satan and his methods. Instead, many pastors prefer to preach positive sermons about Jesus. Mainly because their congregations expect these types of sermons.

Although Jesus's atonement for our sins restored our relationship with God the Father, Christians are at war with an enemy that takes no prisoners. Satan is that enemy, and he is attacking Christians by any means necessary. Satan attacks Christians through deception and with oppressive spirits. These oppressive spirits torment Christians based on their hidden sins or generational curses, whereas nonbelievers are tormented because of their occult activities and sinful lifestyles.

Jesus's sacrifice for our sins also gave us authority over Satan and his demons; however, Christians must be taught how to use this authority. This requires a knowledge of Scripture and how to apply it. In short, knowing how biblical verses apply to given situations. Also, one must have the boldness to confront demonic spirits. This can only occur if a Christian is indwelled by the Holy Spirit.

Many Christians do not understand the purpose of the Holy Spirit. The Holy Spirit is not some mysterious force in the universe. Instead, it's the third person of the Trinity. Although we pray in Jesus's name to cast out demons, it's the power of the Holy Spirit that delivers us. Likewise, it's the inner voice of the Holy Spirit that guides us daily. Therefore, to experience the full blessing and power of the Holy Spirit, you must surrender to him in mind, body, and will.

Full surrender to the Holy Spirit is necessary to fight the snares of the devil because only the Holy Spirit can prepare Christians for spiritual warfare. Given this, Christians cannot be apathetic to the signs of the times.

Therefore, every Christian who is truly saved must be empowered by the Holy Spirit to confront demonic spirits since God expects his children to do his will. One aspect of that will is to exercise authority over Satan and his demons.

Book Excerpt

Like God, Satan has an army of angels too; however, their appearance and authority changed after their banishment from heaven. Thus, demons do not have the same power as angels, but they can still inflict us with physical and mental conditions; moreover, some demons are extremely powerful and rule over nations. Furthermore, unlike angels, demons are meant to hinder not help us. To what extent they hinder us depends on our faithfulness and obedience to the Word. Yes, strong believers will face opposition from demonic forces, but they have the authority in Jesus' name to confront demons.

As noted, most of the attacks of Satan and his demons are against our minds. Satan does this by suggesting bad thoughts to us, and then observing our responses to them. If we don't reject his thoughts immediately, he keeps probing until we accept or reject his temptations. So, Christians must always remember temptation is not a sin, but acting on it would be. Because of this strategy by Satan, Christians should not fear physical manifestations of demons because they are rare. They are rare because God won't allow it. God won't allow it because of the fear factor of seeing demons.

If God restricts how Satan can attack us, can we assume demons cannot appear as men? There is a passage in the Old Testament which seems to confirm demons once walked on the earth as men. In Genesis 6:1–2, we are told about the sons of God taking human wives: Now it came to pass, when men began to multiply on the face of the earth, and daughters were born to them, that the sons of God saw the daughters of men, that they were beautiful; and they took wives for themselves of all whom they chose. No doubt these sons of God were not men. Some contend they were angels, while others say demons. I contend they were demons because God later decides to destroy the world due to its wickedness.

Given the spiritual state of the world today, demons do not need to appear as men because the world is oblivious to the war between Good versus Evil. Fortunately for us, this war is being fought in the spiritual realm. So, in the end time, God and his children will prevail. Right now, though, Christians must have faith and do their part to resist the schemes of the enemy. Because of this, God won't allow demons to deceive the Godly if they are obedient to the Word. Granted, many of the ungodly are being controlled and manipulated by demons, but Christians have the authority in Jesus' name to resist the schemes of the enemy.

Oh God It Hurts

Every day, bad things happen in the world and to good people, and no one can explain why. Religious leaders have different views concerning bad events and evil in the world. Many of these views concern God and whether he has the power to prevent bad things from happening. This book outlines the factors behind bad events and evil in the world.

There are many factors to consider when something bad happens to us or a loved one. The only question is what factor caused the event. Often people want to blame God when bad things happen to them. Yet they ignore the power and influence that Satan has in the world. Although Satan is not omnipresent, he has many demons assigned to individuals and nations. This legion of evil is responsible for many of the bad things that occur in the world.

In addition, our choices and free will are factors to consider when bad things happen to us. God put in place natural and biblical laws for us to follow. When we reject these laws, bad consequences can follow. Yet despite our bad decisions, God is ready to heal our wounds once we place our trust and hope in him.

Another factor that is often overlooked when bad events occur is random chance. Yet this factor is responsible for many of the bad things we experience in life. Furthermore, often we blame God or the devil for random chance bad events. Given this, the believer should always exercise discernment before casting blame on the devil or God for a bad event. Likewise, conceding all things to God is the key to enduring trials in this world.

Book Excerpt

If you are a Christian, you must concede all doubts, worries, and fears to God. Because if you believe that God exists, then he is beyond your understanding. Our minds cannot fully comprehend the majesty of God. If God created the universe, then we are like insects compared to him. Yet, he loves those that love him. Based on this spiritual tenet, how can anyone question him? No doubt there are reasons why God allows Christians to suffer. Nevertheless, it's not our job to determine why. If we are walking in faith daily, God promises to take care of us. Even if that care is to be with us as we utter our last breath.

Conversely, as a Christian, you must concede we have an adversary. That adversary is Satan. I don't think most Christians realize how much Satan hates mankind. Thus, whether you want to ponder it or not, he hates you! Likewise, I don't think many Christians realize the extent of Satan's evil in the world. Because he and his demons are responsible for many of the unspeakable evil acts committed in the world directly or indirectly. Given this, even though the Church is divided over Biblical doctrine, acknowledging Satan as our principal adversary is a tenet that all Christians must agree upon. Jesus tells us clearly in John 10:10 Satan's role and how to overcome his attacks: "The thief does not come except to steal, and to kill, and to destroy. I have come that they may have life, and that they may have it more abundantly."

Although Satan is responsible for many bad things in the world, he cannot be blamed for everything. Satan cannot be everywhere, nor does he have unlimited power. Given this, sometimes bad events occur because of random chance. For example, the collapse of a bridge, an automobile accident, or physical injuries while exercising or at work can all occur without outside influences involved. Also, many of the bad things Christians experience simply happen due to random chance. Likewise, many devastating storms and natural disasters are not caused by God or the Devil. Instead, they are caused by atmospheric factors that cannot be controlled by man.

Because bad things occur because of random chance, believers and nonbelievers will experience these events in their lives. Also, God and the Devil use these events for their purposes. God will use these events to build faith and trust in him. Whereas Satan uses these events to create anger and bitterness towards God. So again, this comes down to your faith and trust in God. The Bible says that faith is the substance of things hoped for, and the evidence of things not seen. When you can view faith in this light, nothing on earth or beneath it can separate you from God's loving arms.